UP FROM THE BOTTOMS

**Autobiographical Reflections of Unexpected
Encounters with Grace:
A Story of Some Challenges, Successes, People and
Choices in My Life**

LEE ROY PITTS, SR.

ISBN:978-0-578-07175-6

Author contact information:

Lee Roy Pitts Sr., PhD.
8016 Corona Avenue
Kansas City, Kansas 66112
913-788-3265

FOREWORD

This is a story about the triumph of God's grace over life's circumstances. Out of the crucible of poverty that Roy experienced comes a strong sense of personal destiny. The sharpness of his mind can be discerned in the detail as he depicts his early childhood and elementary school experiences. His mental capacity was honed by the elementary and secondary teachers he adeptly describes. His love of learning shines through as he relates the various phases of his life. One wonders how he manages to remember the people, places and events of his early years with such clarity.

Anybody who knows Roy personally can attest to the authenticity of his love for his family and for his wife, Eligene. His grown children are a testimony to the careful upbringing which they enjoyed. I am glad to testify that I know Roy Pitts as a friend and teaching colleague. I applaud his ability to rise above life's vicissitudes and see the good in any situation. Where there could justifiably be bitterness and anger, there is the seasoned wisdom of maturity. His journey is testament to the resilience of the human spirit under the grace of God. At the risk of overstating the case, I trust that the reader of this autobiography will gain some insightful truths about life as I did in the reading. I'm reminded of a verse from the song, "Dwelling on the Mountain":

I can see far down the mountain
Where I wondered weary years
Often hindered in my journey
By the ghosts of doubts and fears
Broken vows and disappointments
Thickly sprinkled all the way
But the Spirit led unerring
To the land I hold today
Then the songwriter closes victoriously with the chorus:
Is not this the land of Beulah
Blessed, blessed land of light
Where the flowers bloom forever
And the sun is always bright

Young people, especially young Black people, need to read this autobiography because it will teach you how to rise above your circumstances to make something beautiful of your life. I say "Bravo, Lee Roy Pitts!"

—Edward A. Eddy, Ph.D.

PREFACE

These are personal reflections of some aspects of my life that in some way had an impact on me. They are not the whole of my life, for time and space prohibit such, even if I could recall it all.

Questions asked by my children from time to time and of late, by my grandchildren, served as motivation to write my story. Therefore, I hope these reflections will serve to answer many of their questions and perhaps, some that were not voiced.

Further, my prayer is that this autobiography will be a motivation for my grandchildren and great-grandchildren to come to believe that regardless of circumstances, it is better if they face life from a Biblical faith because they glimpsed the hand of God at work in my life as told in my life story.

I thank my long-time friends, William Bradford Sappington, Howard Dodd, D.D.S., and Edward Eddy, Ph.D., for taking time from busy schedules to read the manuscript and sending helpful suggestions and encouraging remarks.

I thank all four of our children for their encouragement to go forward with writing my story.

A special thanks to our son Eric Wayne Pitts, M.D., and our daughter Jeanette Marie (Gina) Pitts, M.D., for both perusing the manuscript and giving me invaluable suggestions and encouragement. Additional thanks to Gina who, though busy, typed the first draft from my sometimes poor handwriting, due to tired hands.

For her patience with my clutter and being later than ever with chores the last two years, I am grateful to my wife Eligene. You have been the best wife anyone could want through all of this. I promise to try to make up the time to you, Lord allowing.

Finally, Julie Tenenbaum of Final Draft Secretarial Service, I cannot thank you enough. You are indeed the best at your craft. I am so glad our paths crossed. Thanks so much.

He saw Nathanael under the fig tree before He called him. (John 1:48b). He saw me in the Bottoms at the bend of the Kaw river.

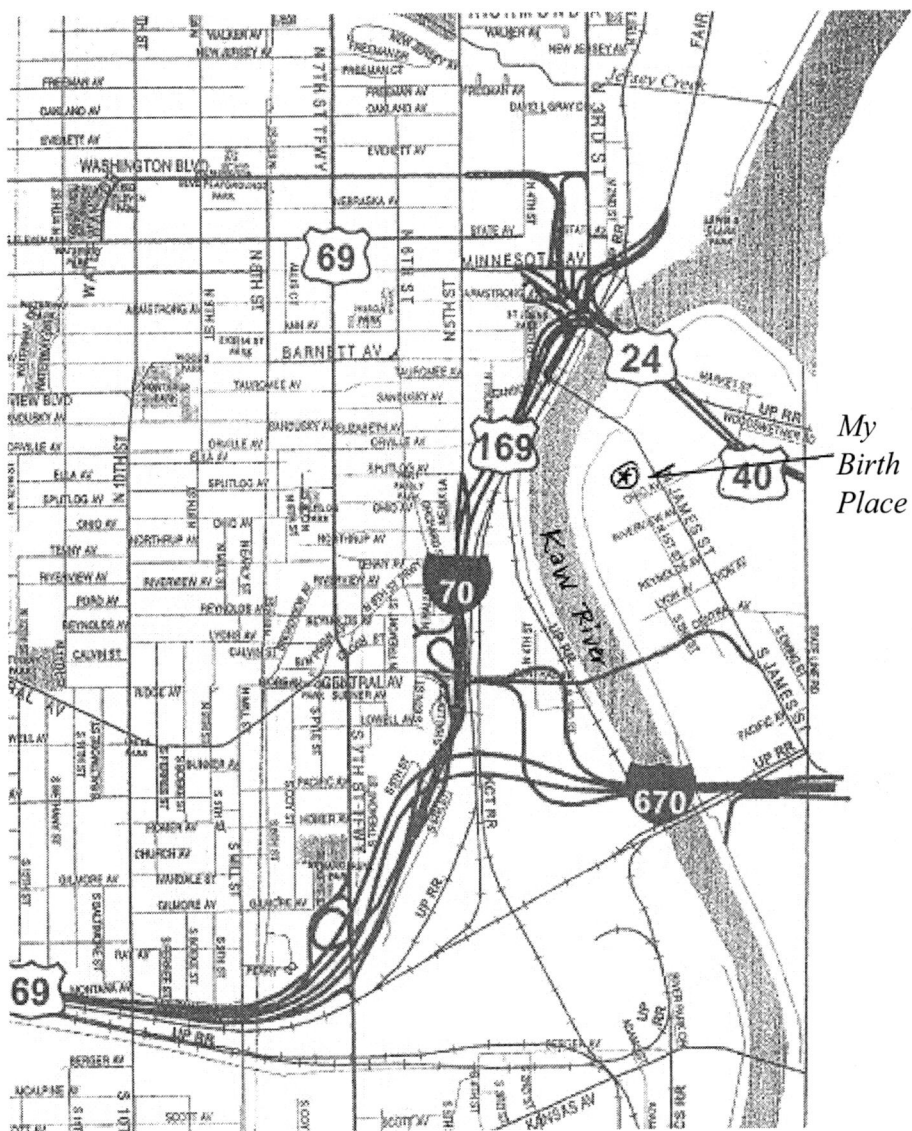

My Birth Place—The West Bottoms, Kansas City, Kansas

Ancestors of Lee Roy Pitts

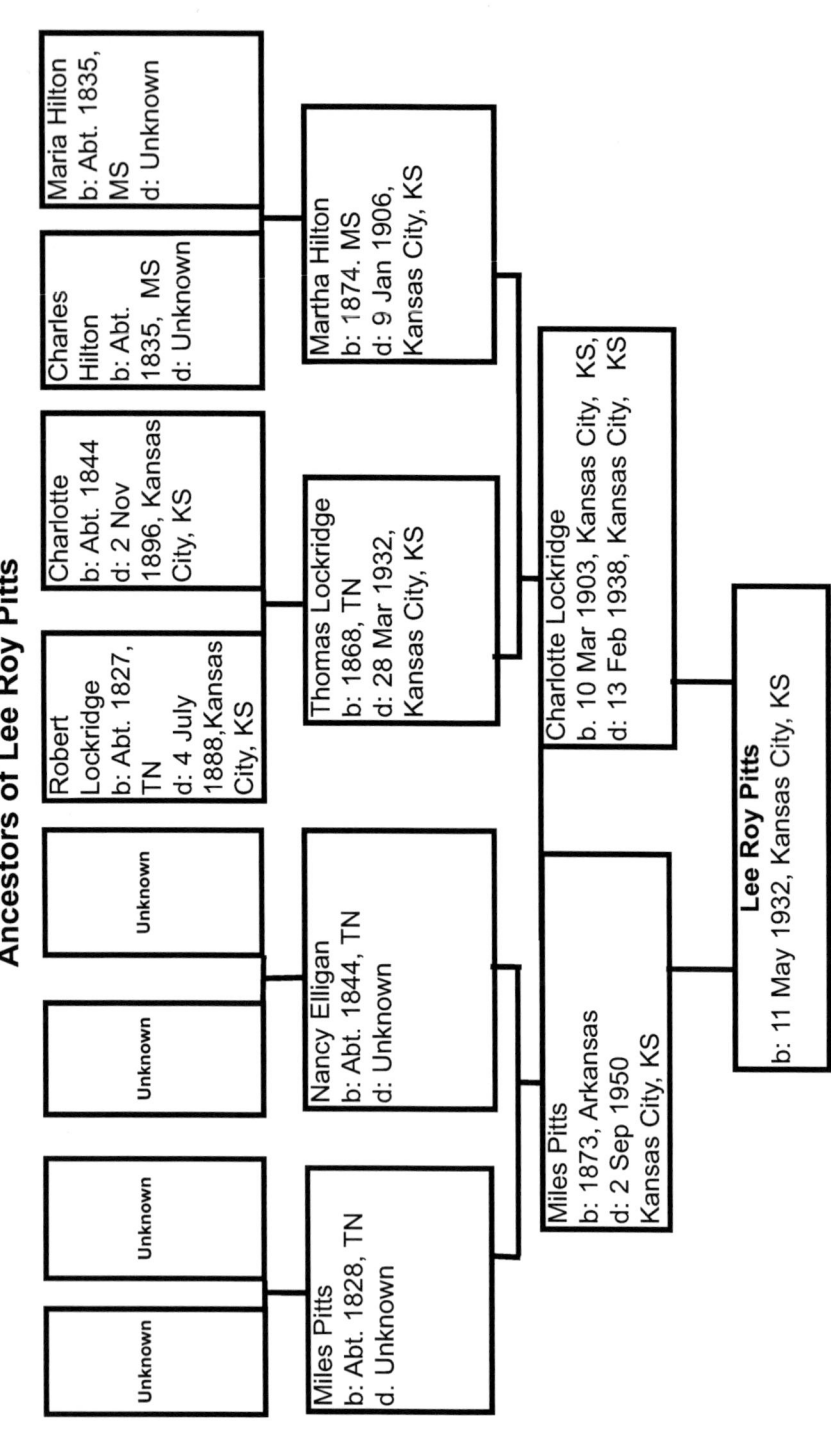

Maria Hilton
b: Abt. 1835, MS
d: Unknown

Charles Hilton
b: Abt. 1835, MS
d: Unknown

Martha Hilton
b: 1874. MS
d: 9 Jan 1906, Kansas City, KS

Charlotte
b: Abt. 1844
d: 2 Nov 1896, Kansas City, KS

Robert Lockridge
b: Abt. 1827, TN
d: 4 July 1888,Kansas City, KS

Thomas Lockridge
b: 1868, TN
d: 28 Mar 1932, Kansas City, KS

Charlotte Lockridge
b: 10 Mar 1903, Kansas City, KS,
d: 13 Feb 1938, Kansas City, KS

Unknown

Unknown

Nancy Elligan
b: Abt. 1844, TN
d: Unknown

Miles Pitts
b: 1873, Arkansas
d: 2 Sep 1950 Kansas City, KS

Unknown

Unknown

Miles Pitts
b: Abt. 1828, TN
d. Unknown

Lee Roy Pitts
b: 11 May 1932, Kansas City, KS

Descendants of Lee Roy Pitts

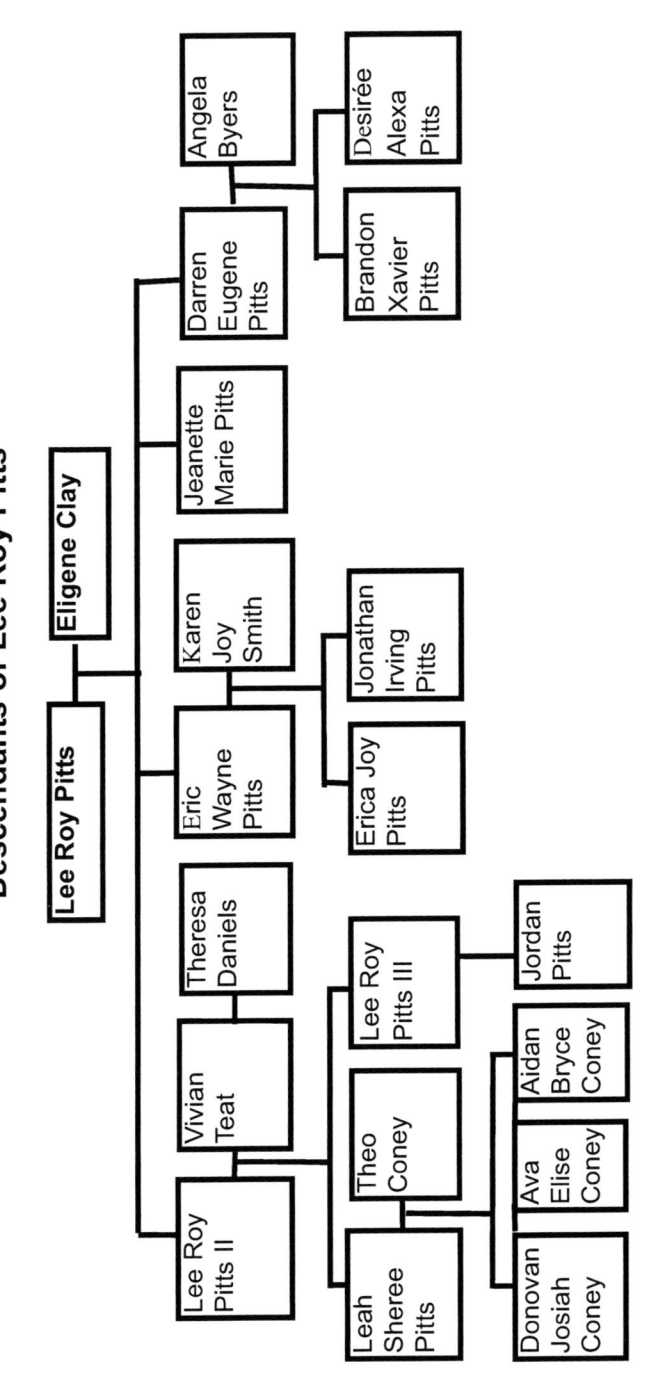

TABLE OF CONTENTS

CHAPTER I

BEGINNINGS

The origin of every person's life is centered in a person and a location. As I think of my beginning, my mind thinks of my mother and the location of my birth. At 6:30 a.m., on May 11, 1932 A.D., the most important person was a sweet Afro-American named Charlotte Lockridge, a professional seamstress - my mother. She pushed me into a journey that up to now has been seventy-seven years. It was a day of beginning for me, but for her the end of her third pregnancy. I was her third pregnancy, her fourth child, and her second son. A fourth pregnancy was to follow me.

My birth took place at 323 North First Street in Kansas City, Kansas. A more modern and technical address, in keeping with our world of satellites, we could say I was born at latitude 39 degrees, seven minutes, 28 seconds and longitude -94 degrees, 36 minutes, 52 seconds. This address is part of a region called Kaw Valley Industrial District in Wyandotte County of Kansas City, Kansas. The name most used by locals and city officials back then was "The West Bottoms." To this date it is referred to in that way.

The main street in this area is Central Avenue. Running perpendicular to Central is the main business street, James Street. Going west towards the river are First and Second Streets. From Central Avenue to the James Street bridge on the northwest end is about 1.5 miles. From James Street to the Kaw river on the west is less than a mile. This small area was to be my home base for sixteen years. But the experience of this area would be with me for a lifetime.

Obviously I do not recall most of what I experienced the first two years. For me, from age three what I recall is suspect as to whether I was three or three and a half. My earliest conscious activity finds me going away from home to get water from a nearby serum plant with my brother Albert (Bud). The plant was around the curve from our house at 323 North First. I was something like three and a half, but not close to four. Even now, in my seventh decade, I remember the incident well. Perhaps because it was my first experience with my brother and because I saw my mother, sisters, and brother laugh so heartily about the incident.

We entered the foyer of a holding plant of Armour Packing Company. This part of the building was a place where hogs and cattle were held for slaughter. A security watchman entered the foyer from another door. He was making the rounds, where at various stations he inserted a large key to indicate all was well at that location. He saw us drawing water, but in doing so our backs were toward him. He said, "What are you doing here?" I became frightened and started running out the door. As I headed home, Bud was calling me and laughing but couldn't run with the water. My brother knew the man was being friendly and that we had permission to get water.

When we got home I recall him telling Momma and my sisters Alberta (Bert) and Madeline (Mat) what happened. They asked me why I ran. I told them he pointed something at us and hollered. While hugging and kissing me, they all were laughing. They knew what I had seen was a key. However, I was scared to death, as we say. This was my earliest recollection, but I had entered the world some three years or so before.

After the "serum plant" incident there are a few others that I recall occurring in the street in front of our house. I remember playing, when it had rained, with a paddle boat that my brother made for me. It had a rubber band on it and would make a flapping noise, mimicking a motor. Then I recall going across the railroad tracks in front of our house to play with William Bradford Sappington ("Sugarman"), who lived on the other side. He was my first friend. My Uncle Alfred lived two doors from Sugarman, so before school age I was going to Sugarman's house and to Uncle Alf's with ease and was unafraid of crossing the tracks.

By the time I was about four, I was much help to my mother. All the other children were of school age, so during the school year, Momma would have me doing things. We lived in a two-story house with three rooms up and three rooms down. We had the downstairs apartment. By the time my baby sister was born in 1935, I recall closing windows or getting a certain pan for Momma.

My mother was bothered with asthma. She would burn a powder of something, and with a towel over her head she inhaled it as much as possible. One night she coughed so hard and so long she had trouble breathing. My brother gave me the substance container and said, "Throw it away." Alberta ran to Aunt Lydia's house. My mother was taken to the hospital that night. The next morning an attendant from Thatcher's Funeral Home knocked on the door. Alberta opened it to hear him say, "They told me to tell the children their mother passed last night." My older sister screamed and my sister Mat was also crying.

It was not long before my mother's sisters, Lydia Love, Martha Burkehead, and the matriarch of our family, my grandfather's sister, Rebecca Vincson (Aunt Beck) all came. Of those three, Aunt Lydia was the only one without children.

With all of us in the middle room, they sat in the front room discussing the situation. I recall them calling Bud and Bert into the front room. While I do not remember all of what was said, I do recall hearing Alberta say to them, "Momma said for us to stay together." Years later, Alberta was surprised that I heard correctly and recalled, though I was only five years old. Alberta concurred with me and filled me in on what was discussed back then. The decision was made to have all of us go to live with Aunt Lydia and her husband, Isom Love. For reasons I do not know, we always called him Mr. Love and never Uncle Isom.

Without doubt the death of my mother was a most stressful event for all of us. Going to Aunt Lydia's was best for us but also was difficult for Evelyn, who was the baby. It broke the attachment to Momma so needed for development during the early months. I am aware of the damage of detachment, but I am also aware that things could have been far worse but for the grace of God working through our Aunt Lydia.

I am thankful that while remembering the negative of Momma's illness and passing, I have fond memories of her sewing for women and men in the neighborhood. I recall all ethnic people came to her. Then I loved when she cooked each of our favorite foods. My favorite was liver and onions with cream style corn or salmon croquettes and cream style corn. Oh! How I recall those times.

My first five years were spent in the vicinity of the 300 block of First Street. My earliest friend, William Bradford Sappington, was born at 2735 Sloan in Quindaro, but very early was brought to live with his maternal grandmother,

Mrs. Lucille Smith at 314 North First Street. At one time, all of my known family members lived in this 300 block. Especially was this true on my mother's side. My maternal grandfather, Thomas Lockridge, left Tennessee and came to Kansas City with his parents and siblings in the late 1870s when he was a child. The only two of his siblings that I knew, Rebecca Lockridge Vincson and Lydia Lockridge Swain, were born after the family's migration to Kansas. In Tennessee the Lockridge family lived in the vicinity of Fisk University. My father was born in Mississippi and went to Arkansas before heading to Kansas City. Both sides of my family arrived in "The Bottoms." So my beginnings in the Bottoms was almost inevitable, since all lived on First Street.

Soon I was school age and was observant and learned to ask questions about the area and especially the people. I do not know when the first non-Indian settlers came into this area. However, I learned that since the latter 1800s and into the 1900s this area became a melting pot of various ethnic groups. During my early years I knew of Afro-Americans coming to the Bottoms, mainly from southern states. Many came from south of the border. Mexicans came from Mexico. Many Europeans were in our area. Then, though fewer in numbers, I knew people from the Caribbean islands who came to the West Bottoms. When we referred to the Bottoms, if it was on the Kansas side, we called it the West Bottoms. If referring to the Missouri side, we called it the East Bottoms. Both were a mix of people, but the West Bottoms had more Afro-Americans and Croatians than the east side. In both the areas, most of the people were usually less well off economically than in other areas. Usually as they improved, they moved from the bottom land. To say these were poor people would be a gross understatement. In the vernacular in our area, we were "po' folks."

The social relations of the area was unusual in what I can best describe as "selective segregation." By this I mean while everyone spoke with all others and worked on jobs with all others, there was for most adults, a social life within their own group, at least for long gatherings. For example, most adult women would talk over the fence daily with other ethnic women, but only on special occasions were there frequent and long visitations in homes of other than their own ethnicity. There was some violation of this where two women got to know and trust and borrow from each other. My Aunt Lydia could break the barriers, and soon she was close with a number of non-Blacks. It was not long before she was in other homes, but this was not the pattern of most adults. With us children, this selective segregation was less true, especially for us boys. We often were in other homes.

Very early I was an observer of human behavior, something I believe is true for most children. Often other boys and I talked about what we saw. There were some people who were very private. They did not wish to be bothered by anyone, regardless of gender, race, or religion, adults or children. Some of them were friendly but still wanted their privacy. They would speak kindly to children when asking you or telling you to leave their property. Then there were those few who desired privacy who also acted and spoke in what we children called "mean." Even with this group we observed two patterns. Some were nicer to children of their race or religion or friends.

By the time we were ten years old, we pretty much knew who was who and what was what in terms of what we could do to remain out of trouble. We had learned the boundaries allowed by most adults. This allowed us to know how to get in "planned trouble," that is, who to harass and how. As contradictory as it may seem to outsiders, the few adults that children thought of as mean, usually had valid reasons for being so. Sometimes "bad" boys had behaved out of the ordinary for boys.

In other words, my experience was that most adults in our area treated us nice when we acted nice and actually looked out for us. Adults would often intervene for children when they were in trouble or doing something wrong. In the Bottoms we never had children molested by adults because there were many adults around always looking. Likewise, there were women who could and would take care of even men had they openly bothered children. Almost every adult knew who each child's parent was and where children lived.

Growing up in this multi-racial environment prepared me well for later years of associating and living in the larger environment. Actually, being raised in this racially mixed society prepared me better in some ways than did the segregated schools that I was to attend. Very early, through observation, interaction, and discussion, I learned much about people in general. For instance, very early I learned that all ethnic groups have some desirable and undesirable behaviors. All have some very intelligent people, some habitual drunks, thieves, some compassionate ones, and all other good and bad traits. No group of people seems to have a monopoly on anything. Having remained in this neighborhood for sixteen years, I find many thoughts and behaviors in myself that emanate from the area. Then sometimes certain thoughts come to mind and I can just about see the person from whom I picked it up. It has been said that many hands are on you as you grow to adulthood. My experience confirms the veracity of this statement.

Schools prepared me academically, but my social interaction growth came first from my family and then from the area in which I grew up.

During the years of the 1920s, 30s, and 40s, survival was tough. It was prior, during, and after the "Great Depression." Frequently in our area, railroad trains carrying coal or wood would pass through the area. It was amazing how racial barriers came tumbling down. There would be Blacks, Mexicans, Polish, Croatians, Italians, and others all uniting to steal this coal or wood, whichever was the goods for the day. Boys and men about sixteen and up would jump (hop) the train and proceed to throw the goods off. Meanwhile, the women would begin moving the wood into stacks. Some carried it home in gunny sacks, and still others placed it on their head. This was an indication of how people can unite in a cause for survival. As unbelievable as it seems, the train conductor-engineer would slow the train, and later would blow the whistle, signaling he was moving on. He allowed folks to get some of the goods.

Little did I know that what I saw was perhaps the greatest unification of Protestants, Catholics, Jews, and all else that I would ever see in my lifetime. I do not think any group believed that taking the coal or wood was in strict accordance or agreement with their religious teaching. Still, all seemed to redefine right and wrong based on the hardship and needs of the moment. The next day most of the adults would have stopped any of us children if they saw us stealing. When the blessings were said at the supper table, there was thanks even for the wood or coal. For our families it was like "manna from heaven."

Yet somehow, even in this complex situation of learning when to do what and what boundaries to cross and not to cross, most of us handled it well.

The main occupation for most of the people was working at one of the many "packing houses." These were slaughterhouses where livestock, usually cattle or hogs, but sometimes sheep or others, were killed daily. There was one place they killed horses for a few years when I was about ten years old. It was across from our house. My uncle said he didn't like horse meat, but my aunt bought some and cooked it. That evening we were all quiet as we watched my uncle eat more than his share. We were cracking up laughing as we watched Aunt Lydia muffle her laugh. Later he couldn't believe it was so good with the gravy she made.

At these slaughterhouses, hourly workers could make a good living, so many women and men sought work in these noted houses like Armour, Cudahy, Swift, and other less well known ones.

There was one great drawback that I later saw. In working for these companies, quite often after junior high school, young boys would drop out of school for good to make the good money. Family hardship was sometimes a legitimate reason for working, but too often it was lack of maturity and the inability to see the value of high school for the road ahead. Admittedly there were times when boys were motivated, but the lure of money now made it easier to quit.

Since the Bottoms was zoned for heavy industry, there were a number of such companies affording work. Two of note were I. J. Cohen and Sonken Galamba, scrap iron companies that hired a number of men and women. Much of the work in these companies was physically hard and dangerous. I personally know this, since my Uncle Isom Love worked for I. J. Cohen. They had large cutting shears, machines that could cut large pieces of metal when it was placed between two cutting edges. One blade was stationary while the other moved up and down, like scissors. I was there one day with my uncle's lunch and while waiting for the lunch whistle to blow, I watched him at work. His hand was caught on a piece of metal, and he lost two fingers. He was working the Big Shear. None of the other workers would work the Big Shear, and only a few would work the Little Shear. It was hard and dangerous work.

Then I watched my cousin, Emmett Lockridge, working at Eldridge Packing House, pick up a quarter of beef, remove it from a cooler, and place it in a truck. That was called "lugging beef." The truck in turn delivered meat to stores.

Another interesting but dangerous job I saw very early was the icing of railroad refrigeration cars. These were box-cars on the train tracks that carried meat from slaughter-houses to distant cities. On each end of the boxcar were holes where ice could be placed. Large ice trucks with beds that could be lifted up, carried ice to the top of the train car. There men would unload the ice and push it into the holes. Often men would let ice "accidentally on purpose" fall to the ground for the people below. I did not know of anyone with a refrigerator. We had iceboxes.

A number of men worked for the railroad doing common labor. The pay was very good, and the railroad retirement plans were better than most jobs. I learned this from several men in our neighborhood and an older man I called Bro Denny. He was a member of our church; his full name was Elijah Denny, and he worked for the Santa Fe railroad. Men like Bro Denny and one named Mr. Crudup, with less skill and education, worked in the rail yards setting new rails, cleaning out freight cars, or repairing the Pullman coaches of passenger trains.

You would expect the less educated to be applying for and doing the hard physical work found in the jobs mentioned above. However, during those times of few jobs in other areas, plus racial segregation, there would be educated and uneducated applying for jobs at these plants. An example, though the work may be an upgrade from others, is the Postal Service. Many were the times in the 1930s, 1940s, and up through the 1950s, when there were Black lawyers working at the Post Office. I also knew several that were degreed other than in law.

Everyone felt the economics of the times, but due to segregation, Black men, in my opinion, suffered more. My father, John Miles Pitts, was skilled in the craft of brick masonry, but coming north, he could not become a member of the union. That meant he could not work for a company. As a preteen and early teenager, I was exposed to the jobs I mentioned. I knew one doctor personally, Dr. Braithwaite, and I knew about a train engineer, but I never visualized attaining those as life work.

CHAPTER II

OHIO ENVIRONMENT: AUNT LYDIA'S HOUSES

When we moved to Aunt Lydia's at 10 Ohio Street, my world of observation really expanded. I had been used to the shotgun house of my birth on First Street, where most homes were one story and of wood construction. Now at 10 Ohio we lived in a huge two-story house on an alley. It was a half block from James Street. On James Street, Central Avenue and State Line, almost all businesses were of brick construction. Our new home had a large kitchen, one large bedroom, and one large front or living room, all upstairs. There was water in the kitchen but no indoor toilet facility.

It was at this house that I played with children other than Bill Sappington. Living downstairs was a Mexican family, the Adrianos. We came to be very close to this family. Their mother was Miss Vera and their father was Mr. Frank. My aunt was extremely close to Miss Vera, and it was apparent how much they depended on each other. Aunt Lydia was the older of the two. Their children were Angelina, Frank, Reuben, Joey, and Anita, in that order. Angie was a beautiful girl with a beautiful smile who was good friends with my sister Mat. Frank was nice looking and Sugarman's and my age.

There was a very large yard in which all of us kids

played. This house had two large sheds in which we stored wood, coal, and any other storage material. All over the Bottoms livestock was permitted, and the Adrianos and Aunt Lydia had chickens. They had several goats.

As on First Street, railroad tracks ran down Ohio. So when we first moved to 10 Ohio Street, I was five and was not allowed to play in the street unless Alberta, Bud, or Mat was out there with me. As Sugarman and I got older, around perhaps third or fourth grade, we went further from home and played with more children. When we were young, the trains were to be avoided because of their danger. By the time we were fifteen, we learned to hop slow-moving trains or one standing still and go to the other side of the road. Only older men would hop fast moving trains. As I look back, I know God had mercy on children and fools.

Some of my most cherished preteen memories were in the neighborhood of 10 Ohio Street. I observed much and grew in many ways, not to mention the fun I had with children my age. It was after entering the homes of friends in this neighborhood that I noticed that in other families, food was often prepared differently than in my home. At such a young age to me it seemed, but for that difference, we were mostly alike. I did not notice anyone with much more economically until around early teens.

In this area my sisters played jacks with other girls, jumped rope in the yard or street, and played ball in the street with us boys. My sister Mat was very good at ball playing, while my sister Alberta was not. We, the boys, made rubber guns, slingshots that we called bean shooters, and shot marbles. I was a fair marble shooter, but my brother was extremely good, as was my best friend, Sugarman.

One game we played very early at 10 Ohio Street was a game called "sheeny." We learned sheeny from our

European neighbor's boys. It was like hockey, only played with a tin can and some type of club to hit the can. Two teams each tried to hit the can to the opposite end of the playing field. Our field was usually the street or a vacant lot that had been cleared. But more than any game played from about eight years to about eleven or twelve was what we called runaway. Someone was "it," and he had to catch and tag other boys. When a boy approached you, you would ask him if he was "it" or had been tagged or caught yet. He was to let you know. If he was, you took off running. This went on until everyone was caught or time ran out. We set boundaries where we could run and set time when the game was over. I recall we ran for what seemed like hours. What fun we had. I was very good at anything that required running, so runaway was one of my favorites.

When I talk with Bill Sappington, he also talks about those times and games with the same nostalgic fond memories of our childhood. During that time I never called him Bill. He was always Sugarman. His grandmother called him Sugarman when he was just a baby. To this day to all of us who lived in the Bottoms, he is Sugarman. My very close friends called me Pete. Sugarman and I were both "Guy," but only between us. Often, like in any area, nicknames flourished more than people's real names. Sometimes real names were lost.

We knew real people with names like Cy, Shoe, Pooky, Dump, Chubby, Hot, Badeye, Doteye, Tenfoot Anna, Shug, Hoggie, and these people answered to these names. Some of these were Caucasian, Afro-American, some children, and some adults. The humor about it all was that if they were adults, we had to say "Good morning, Mr. and Mrs. so and so."

For example, I recently learned that the person my aunt called Hot was a man whose name was Bill Puskavich. To us children he was Mr. Hot, while to adults he was Hot. I do not know his specific ethnicity, only that he was a Caucasian married to a beautiful Black woman named Mrs. Tomasine. I do know that he was a respectful man we liked. He chewed "Day's Work" tobacco, and his jaw was always so pushed out he looked like Dizzy Gillespie, the musician. It was at their house I saw my first TV. I was about seventeen years of age, and it was a small TV sitting on the porch. They invited us into the yard to see it.

Nicknames were used so much that at times Bill and I now as seniors have to call each other to ask what someone's real name is. We laugh about it. Recently, I was looking in the telephone book for Poncho Adriano, a close childhood friend. I must have looked for three minutes before it came to mind that I was looking for Frank Adriano. To us he was always Poncho. Such was the impact of nicknames in our area.

We lived at 10 Ohio for about four years after mom's passing. It was a happy time after a while, because we seem to have gotten closer as children. My brother and oldest sister were twins. Their names were Albert and Alberta Rice. To us they were Bud and Bert. Our mother was married first to their dad, a Mr. Rice. At this Ohio address Bud and Bert took over watching and teaching me, along with my Aunt Lydia. My sisters Madeline and Bert got very close. I got closer to my brother. He taught me how to cut wood safely and to use a two-man saw to saw railroad crossties. He taught me a lot about what not to do and what to do. In winter we did all of the work inside the shed. He was the one that earlier before mom passed had taken me to Uncle Alf's before age three. He was an exceptionally good artist and often would draw comic pictures to make me laugh. He was the one who got me interested in art. Also I have fond memories of helping him make a kite and then going with him to the river to fly it. So even with an age difference of seven years, our emotional bond became very strong. It was strong enough to cause great emotional hurt a few years later when I heard he had been killed in action. He went down with the USS Indianapolis, a heavy cruiser that delivered part of the atomic bomb to the island of Tinian in the Pacific ocean.

Another reason I was happy when living at 10 Ohio Street was because I started school from that house and I enjoyed school. I did well at Grant Elementary School and formed a number of friendship bonds with boys and girls. I felt very much a part of the classes and felt most of the students liked me. When teamwork or games were going on, I always tried to be involved. Many of my classmates knew my Aunt Lydia, who made every PTA meeting. Our principal, Mr. D. W. (Daniel Webster) Lewis, often asked me how Mrs. Love was, many years later. So I am sure I did well in grade school because I had good relations with and liked my classmates and my teachers, and therefore worked harder. All of those were stimuli for success.

Last, I enjoyed this period because I began building friendships apart from my family and my best neighborhood friend, Sugarman. However, even with him our relations got stronger and were foundational to our developing trust that was to come in handy during our pre-military teen years. We were always there, as early as beginning days; there to talk about things. It ended up with a kind of "having each other's back" thing. During those preteen years I am sure we did not fully know how important our friendship would be at a later time.

After about four years at 10 Ohio, when I was around nine years old, Aunt Lydia moved to the other end of the Bottoms, first to 24 North Second, and later to 9 North Second. The house at 24 North Second was a nice two-story house. We lived upstairs, and a family called the Kemps lived downstairs. They had a number of girls and one boy named Clyde who was in my class. One girl named Dorothy was in my sister Mat's class. Their baby sister was a girl named Emma, and she and my baby sister Evelyn were classmates. They were wonderful people, and we grew to like their mom and dad. He drove a pretty and large automobile. They soon moved across the bridge and out of the Bottoms, to where they would be nearer schools and a better environment.

It was then that the Dodd family moved upstairs and we had moved down. This family would forever be an integral part of our lives. Other than my relatives, this was the first time I became bonded to an entire family like brothers and sisters. In other situations I was bonded more to one member of the family. However, these girls were really like my sisters and the boys were like my brothers. Their mom, Juanita, affectionately called Miss Lottee, and their dad, affectionately called Mr. Taft, were just wonderful. They all loved my Aunt Lydia, and like us, called her Aunt Lydee. My aunt dearly loved them also. In her senior years, Miss Lottee often looked after her.

Their oldest son Howard and I became good friends, and that bond is even stronger today. He was in my wife's and my sister Evelyn's class, the 1953 class of Sumner High School. He is a graduate of Kansas State University and Meharry Medical College in Dentistry. He rose to the rank of bird Colonel in the Army National Guard. To this date, Howard is one of my cherished friends and one of the most intellectually and emotionally balanced persons I have known.

I am glad my children got to know Howard long before they went off to college. They learned how much Eligene and I love and respect him and his family. As youngsters, they greeted him with esteem in their voices as they said "Hi, Dr. Dodd."

Howard's family soon moved to the larger part of Wyandotte County just before we moved down the street to 9 North Second Street, one of two houses my uncle purchased. Neither house had any conveniences other than a roof that leaked something awful, we were soon to discover. One of my wishes at the time was that we would have had the wisdom to follow the Kemps, Dodds, and others to the environment closer to the schools we attended. To have done so would have brought so many more advantages to us children in the academic preparation sense, and motivation. The advantages in the Bottoms were more for adults and young boys who could thrive in a country-like environment.

If you were a boy growing up in the West Bottoms section of Kaw Valley, there were assets and dangers. We had some fun that we couldn't have experienced elsewhere in the city. By the time I was eight, we were catching pigeons and swapping them. Silver Kings (pure white) were some of the preferred. We would sometimes find them nesting under bridges and near box cars that were carrying grain. We also made bean shooters, which were upgraded slingshots of the ancient world of the Bible times. Ours were more accurate than back then. We practiced by setting up tin cans in a vacant lot or down on the riverbank. No one said anything, as long as we didn't shoot houses or people. It was like living on the farm in the country. There was plenty of space to run.

Sometimes we went to the stockyards and milked cows that were there to be slaughtered. My brother Albert and my cousin Melvin Burkehead first took me when I was around nine and showed me how to ride. They would find one at the feeding trough and let me sit on it. By the time I was thirteen other boys and I were pretty good at riding cows. I do not know of any girls riding cows, but they would go with us early in the morning to milk cows. My sister Madeline was good at milking, but Alberta never learned the art of milking. Interesting that both of them could be a lady, but I think Alberta was just too scared to try to milk.

Thinking about the dangerous things we did, another comes to mind. We would see the older boys and young men swim the river out to the first pier. Some would jump into the river from the bridge. Young boys who could not swim as yet would get a large piece of cork, wrap a man's belt around it and themselves, and use it as a float to get to the pier. I recall seeing this done and was tempted to do it. But I recall before age ten my brother and cousin Melvin told me never to go into the river until I could swim. But after my brother left when I was ten, I do recall going in one time near Twin Bridges rather than the James Street bridge. Bill Sappington seems to recall us doing it more than once. Since he learned to swim before me, I suspect he did it a number of times with Poncho and others. In any event, after a friend of ours named Junior Cobb drowned, I never went to the river again. However, with no swimming pools and weather being hot, one can see the temptation for us boys. Now in my senior years, my nerves quiver when I think what could have happened to us who took those chances.

Those of us who got by are living testimonies that God has mercy on fools and babies, and in some ways we were both. We experienced unexpected encounters with grace.

At 24 North Second Street, our circle of friends soon widened. I came to know other children whose parents knew the adults in my family. There was the Sanders family of Marian, James, William, Bobby, and Clarice. Then there were the Robinsons - Betty, Shirley, and William. These families were so close to us that I always knew if I was up to something wrong, don't be around the adults in those families. They had the right to chastise us on the spot and like any other adult, would send a message home.

It was at Second Street that I met one of the most talented families in our area. It was the Walkers. Their mother, Mrs. Essie, was a sweet little lady, and her children were Maxine, Odom, Artemis, Marjorie, and Norman. If I would select one family on the basis of ability, it would certainly be the Walkers. Yet none of them completed high school. They came from Oklahoma shortly after we moved to Second Street. Recently Maxine related to me some of the internal strife that ensued because of her dad. This kind of irresponsibility, while existing everywhere, was too apparent in our area. So many of us from the Bottoms fell through the cracks because of that obstacle.

One family that was replete with abdication of parental responsibility was a family I will let remain nameless and call Family X. One boy was in my class. Very early he was a troubled boy. Then a younger boy followed his behavior, and in some ways took bad behavior to another level. Sad to say, when we were children, we noticed that a number of the men and women in that family were prone to violence. But as is often the case, there were a few who in later life changed and sought to save the others from the pattern of violence.

When I think of these families and others, words cannot adequately state how much talent went undeveloped in the

Bottoms and how many of us were shortchanged because of family discord and general environment not beneficial for children academically.

Our house at 24 North Second was a much better house. It was closer to I. J. Cohen Scrap Iron Company where my uncle worked. Regardless of the reason for moving, it was a move up for me, as it did much for my growing self esteem. I think it was around my last grade school years, and I had become aware of material differences in families. This new house had electricity, water, and indoor toilet facilities. At the previous house we had a couple of rooms with electricity and water, but no indoor facility for necessary needs.

On entering the house, we were all excited. There was a living room, dining room, one bedroom, a kitchen, and bath. There was a front and back porch with a shed or garage for storage.

Boy, I thought, no more metal tubs for baths behind the curtain like cowboys. I tell you, my days were getting better in my youthful mind. I felt good because for the first time in my life, I wouldn't mind when someone other than my best friend came to visit us. I never wanted everything, but had matured enough to want improvement.

This apparent move up in the world lasted only a short time. My uncle decided to become an owner of real estate. It was a good idea for his needs, but I wasn't ready for it, and no other family member wanted it, including my aunt. The two houses he purchased had three rooms each, no water, no electricity, no foundation, and a leaking roof. Immediately, he had to borrow money to repair the roof. Many rainy days we had buckets to catch water. I was not the only one to feel a letdown. However, I soon reluctantly got used to carrying a lamp from room to room and to the outdoor facility at night. I never invited anyone to our house that wasn't from the Bottoms.

It may have been immaturity on my part, but as I look back, even now I believe I was a normal sixth or seventh grader. When it comes to basic needs, I think most children, when once exposed, want what other children possess. Such perception reaches into children's behavior. I have seen children of divorced parents hurt because they no longer live in the family home. Often they will pretend or lie about what they have.

Again, we have reasons why William Bradford Sappington and I are such good friends. He too had similar experiences. As a result, we were both in each other's homes without embarrassment. It was known that neither would nor could we make fun or look down on the other, because our boats were in the same stream. Our situations were so similar that on leaving the Bottoms, we just hung together.

Later in life when we were more perceptive and mature, we learned that many of our classmates who did not live in the West Bottoms were experiencing similar degrees of poverty. During our tender years, we do not know that all perception is not reality. Much of what we thought we saw was deceptive. I recall going to visit a classmate. Stepping into the living room, I felt out of place. I actually thought they were so far ahead of me that I could not date their daughter. What I didn't know was they were wise enough to fix up the front living room and took their time with the rest of the house.

Before we moved from 24 North Second to the two sub-standard houses, my older brother and sister left home to live on their own. They were seventeen years of age and had problems with my uncle. Their leaving brought about many changes. After Albert left, all of the outdoor work became my responsibility. I had worked with him since I was six years of age. As I grew in size and strength, he taught me more complex jobs. By the time I was eight, I was cutting wood with a double blade axe. Very early I had learned and cultivated a work ethic as both of us worked at Uncle Alf's house.

My brother was drafted into the Navy during World War II. It was while we were still at 24 North Second that we received word that he was missing in action, followed several days later by a telegram saying he was killed in action. From that time, I missed a lot of playing because even though our energy source in winter was coal, I needed to find wood for heat when there was no coal. For cooking we used wood in winter and summer. There were times I had to go find wood. I eventually discovered a factory on the Missouri side that made wooden boxes. The scraps were left over from the boxes they threw away. I would go there and get wood. A man named Mr. Swanson made me a wagon. It was very balanced, so when it was loaded it was easy to push or pull. The wheels had ball bearings and thick grease. During the summer months after I brought two loads home I could sell wood.

As usual, Uncle Alf always helped me by purchasing a load or two. As I said, I missed a lot of playing and teen activity, such as ball games that often occurred on the Cooper school ground. Cooper was a school that had once been used but was torn down during our time. Then it was just a large flat dirt field. Some days I would stop with my load and watch part of an inning before moving on to get another load.

I made quite a bit of money. I gave it to my aunt to help with clothes for my two sisters still at home. I always wanted my sisters to look good, since they usually left on

Sundays to visit some of my dad's other children. Then since all I did was work, I thought all I needed was work pants. This view soon changed when I got well into junior high. There I started wanting to look good.

CHAPTER III

SPIRITUAL ROOTS

With all that we did that was typical of children, always we had the influence of the church in one form, type, or the other. My earliest church attendance was at a little church called Rising Star Baptist Church. It was located at First and Ohio Street, one-half block from Aunt Lydia's house and one block from my birth home. The pastor when I was a child was Reverend Fred Williams, and his wife was Catherine. They had no children but seemed to like children. They were good friends of my aunt and uncle, and this was the only church we attended then. I knew of no other Protestant church in Kaw Valley. All others had long since moved across the bridge. We were the only children in attendance most of the time.

I have to admit they tried to do things to hold our attention and sometimes did so. At Christmas or Easter we all had speeches, which my sisters Alberta and Madeline usually wrote. Then each year there was a drawing contest which we always knew my brother was going to win, and Mat would be second. Neither of us was as good as Bud. His drawings looked like photos.

For the larger community they had fish fry dinners periodically. We enjoyed these because it was a change from our having adult company for dinner on Sunday, when we waited until after the reverend and wife ate. Our best dinners were usually on Sunday, so waiting was not something we looked forward to. Such was the case so often that I made a promise to myself that if I ever had children, they would eat with adults or first. To this day it still bothers me to go to a church social or dinner and all the adults are in line and the little children are waiting.

In spite of the perceived negatives of this church, the positives outweigh them. On a personal level, Reverend Williams was one of the finest persons ever to visit our home. He worked full time at Paul Kaiser Packing House. I do not recall them doing evangelism like going to houses for new members or inviting people to the church. However, they were a positive in our neighborhood as a spiritual house of worship and people who cared. They allowed funerals of people who were not members. Though few of the deacons were well educated, they were always dressed well and spoke without foul language. They treated us children with respect and love. From that perspective, they did more with less than many today do with greater knowledge and more materially.

I attended this church off and on during my preteens. Their next pastor was Reverend Johnson and his wife. They had children: one girl was about three years my junior. She passed shortly after graduation from high school. They were all very nice people, and the last time I saw them I was on furlough. The church had moved out of the Bottoms to Walker Avenue between Tenth and Eleventh Street. I often drive by there and give thanks just because some of these early members were in my life and memory.

Rising Star was the last Protestant church in the Kaw Valley area and the only church that was there for years since the Catholic church had long since left the area.

Shortly after our mother passed in 1938, we began

attending church with my Aunt Ada, the wife of my mother's brother, Alfred Lockridge. She was a member of the Church of God located at 1060 Freeman in Kansas City, Kansas. My attendance there increased, and my attendance at Rising Star became sporadic. I recall going to that church in a long old funeral hearse that Sugarman just told me was a Packard. It was owned by a man we called Mr. Senior Smith. My aunt and my classy big sister were embarrassed to roll up to the church in this old, large black hearse. My sister Mat, while not preferring it, was a little indifferent. I, being young and silly at five and six, thought it was fun. How I remember thinking we are different and people will now notice us. They did. We only road in the hearse when my uncle's old car would not start after cranking or he would be angry with Aunt Ada and wouldn't let her drive. My brother always stayed with Uncle Alf, so I do not remember him going to Freeman Avenue Church.

This church did a lot of outreach and home visitation evangelism. They did so as long as it could be done without going into places like saloons or where they had to mingle for long with "sinners." They didn't visit churches much other than their own denomination or group. When I asked my Aunt Lydia why she didn't go with us, she said she had gone there some time ago. She did not like their attitude because they came across as if they were the only church teaching truth. She thought them to be judgmental and so did not go back.

When I returned from military service, the topic came up again. We were discussing beliefs and speaking about something similar that came up at her church, Pleasant Green Baptist Church. She said it different, but it had the same meaning. She said, "Folks who put folks in heaven or hell don't have one square inch of heaven to keep me out and they don't have one square inch of hell to put me in." Aunt Lydia had only gone to the eighth grade at the old Bruce School in the Bottoms around 1898. Blacks couldn't go any further. She only had an eighth grade education, but my, how she could reason.

During those years the teaching of that church was the belief that God had a spiritual standard, and it included a lot of don'ts. You don't smoke, drink, go to movies, dance, and on and on with what they considered to be the correct application of Scripture. Whatever they considered wrong became distinctive marks that a Christian ought not do. I must add that they were not alone during that time in that practice. During that time, many churches, I have learned, were into that kind of practice. Often, they were referred to as "holiness churches." Many, if not most, of them have revisited what some call pharisaical tendencies, and are more in line with mainline Christian beliefs or a more balanced view, a more Biblical take on the true marks of a Christian. As a result, some fellowships have widened.

Regardless of the actual and perceived shortcomings of that church, it, like the Rising Star Baptist, contributed to my moral development and provoked my thinking about spiritual matters. Looking back, even as a youngster I could see errors in their thinking. However, with all the pull of the streets on youngsters then and now, I found great benefit in focusing on the why of their teaching rather than their extreme methods of being holy people. It was their teaching that led me to some decisions that spared me from many unwanted consequences.

I do not recall going to Freeman Church of God on a regular basis when I got old enough to rebel against church. That probably was the mid-teens - a mistake.

There were a number of times Aunt Ada did not have use

of the car. Some of those times we went to other churches with Aunt Lydia. Aunt Martha Burkehead and her husband, Uncle Johnny, would pick us up, and we would go to Shiloh Baptist, Pleasant Green Baptist, and less frequently, Metropolitan Baptist. All of these were where some family member on my mother's side was a member. My oldest great aunt and the matriarch of our family, Rebecca Vincson, was a member of Metropolitan Baptist, and her husband was an associate pastor there for a number of years.

My sisters Alberta and Madeline and I thought we went often to Shiloh because Aunt Lydia was good friends with the pastor and his wife. It was true that Reverend and Sister Fisher were friends with not only Aunt Lydia but our entire family. However, greater still, years later I was called by my cousin Helen Burkehead, who stated that she had been at an anniversary program at Shiloh. There, to her surprise, our grandfather, Thomas Lockridge, was listed as one of the founders. We were so pleased, and that answered our earlier wonderings of why we went there so often.

Miles Pitts, my father, had two sets of children before starting a family with my mother. All of them except one sister became members of Strangers Rest Baptist Church with my dad. Even cousins followed him to the church. This church is special to me for another reason. One of the former pastors, Reverend C. A. Pugh, was my grade school weekday church school pastor. Then he was pastor at First Baptist Church at Fifth and Nebraska. We attended there every Wednesday.

Reverend Pugh always gave concluding remarks. He became the second highly educated Black male to make an impact on me. In retrospect, I believe he was so aware of speaking to impressionable youth that he was careful to maximize the opportunity. I was moved not only by what he said but also by the manner in which he related to us. Even in the fifth and sixth grade I could detect a realism with him. I left feeling that he really cared if we learned as well as how we behaved. Reverend Pugh was a well dressed man with a three-piece suit and a gold chain connected to a watch in the breast pocket of his vest. I am glad I got a chance to share my thanks with him when he was pastor of Strangers Rest Baptist.

While none of my family members attended the Church of God in Christ, very early I did learn something of their faith traditions. As a preteen and early teen, I would slip in back of the little storefront "church" headed by two ladies. They called it a mission church. These ladies were affectionately called Momma Minnie and Aunt Sis. Their services were full of emotion and live music. If you were outside you might think at least ten or so people would be inside, when actually most of the time it would be three to five. There was always Aunt Sis, Minnie Moss (Momma Minnie), their brother, and a little old man they called Bro Loveless. Bro Loveless was known to visit folks' homes around supper time. If you asked him if he would have dinner, his famous words were, "I believe I will, I believe I will." Most folks got to know him and put a stop to his bumming, as the old folks called it. He played a banjo.

Aunt Sis and Momma Minnie raised a classmate of mine named Joseph Garcia - to us he was DD. They raised him and looked after stray kids. I have fond memories and respect for these ladies, with all their peculiarities in dress. I shudder to think of where some children would have been without their commitment.

As a senior now, age wise, I am thankful to have been exposed to a few of the religious views of the day. They went far in helping me to formulate where I am today. Though I worked for some Jews and Catholics as a child, I was not exposed to the inner workings of those faith traditions. The same is true of Mohammedans, though they were in the Bottoms. Later in life I did study some of these faiths and was privy to some great minds like Maimonides and others.

The latter part of 2008 I received a call from a childhood friend. He was finally released from incarceration, where he had been since about 1950. After speaking with him, I discovered that he was released due to illness. In grade school he had a sharp mind. At least several other times I had corresponded with him. Over the years he unfortunately had not yet arrived at the point where he could see the benefit of religious thinking. He told me that since being imprisoned he had completed high school and then a few other courses. His thinking reminded me of the scripture that says, "They are ever learning but never coming to the knowledge of the truth." I pray that the Lord has mercy on him as he did me in my ignorance when I rejected him.

My early exposure to church life helped me as a teenager to live within certain limits. I became aware that while not being perfect, by living within some limits, I was saved from much wayward and non-beneficial behavior. To come to that reasoning of mind early itself was nothing short of an unexpected encounter with God's grace. Spiritual teaching helps to ease many of life's burdens when known and when practiced. When I became an adult I accepted the Christian faith as my way of life.

There are two ladies and their husbands who, putting their faith into action, were a great help to me. What they did encouraged me when I was an early teen. Their behavior made my perceived and actual struggle bearable.

To understand the benefit of what these ladies did for me, one needs to be acquainted with what was happening at the time. The context was my brother left home when he was seventeen and was immediately drafted into the U.S. Navy. Later he was killed during World War II. It was then that the outside work of cutting wood, sawing wood, bringing in coal, and feeding the livestock all became chores of mine exclusively. I was about ten when he left home and twelve when we received word that he was killed in action. Before he left home, we had worked together. After he left, my social life such as playing was greatly diminished. I seldom had time to go anywhere. This is where the two ladies impacted my life.

Mrs. Niona Butler McConnall and her husband Houston asked my aunt if they could take me with them to Memorial Hall. They took me to a wrestling match and to eat. While a wrestling match to most people would not be an important event, and it did not enhance my intellect, their purpose was achieved. They recognized the need of a youngster to have a change from an axe to an outlet just for fun. They're in my memory, and I have told them so many times.

Then several summers I got a chance to go to Bonner Springs to visit a friend of my aunt, Mrs. Hattie Ross. Mrs. Ross had a niece named Ludie, later Mrs. Ludie Wills. She married a World War II army veteran, Ersie Wills, who became a Baptist minister. The Wills took me to their home and he showed me how to shoot a rifle and hike. He had brought a Carbine rifle home after the war. Before Ludie married, I had a number of good days because in Bonner Springs at 241 Springdale, she taught me many things about country living that we did not do in Kaw Valley. I had a good time working with her.

Recently, after a number of years not knowing her location, I found Mrs. Wills. I went to her church to worship with her at Jerusalem Baptist Church on Tenth here in Kansas City, Kansas. At her church when I was introduced I stood and shared what this Christian lady meant to me because when I was a teenager she spent time listening to and taking time with me. She still had a Mona Lisa smile that would have been the delight of Norman Rockwell to paint.

Later Eligene and I visited this fine Christian octogenarian lady in her home. I am so glad that she saw many years come and go without loss of that look of peace in her soul, a look I first saw in my teens. The blessing was mine to have thanked her for her Christian love in action.

CHAPTER IV

REFLECTIONS ON SOME SCHOOL EXPERIENCES: ELEMENTARY

Upon reflecting on school days, I find that from the very beginning to now I loved school and learning. Without doubt much of my love of learning came from the early experiences given to me by my grade school teachers and principal. To all of them I am so grateful.

All of my elementary school years were spent at Grant Elementary School. It was located at Fourth and Everett in Kansas City, Kansas. It went from kindergarten to sixth grade. The principal was Mr. Daniel Webster Lewis. He was called D. W. (or Daniel Boone behind his back). I did not get to really know him until fifth grade and more in the sixth grade when he taught our class for half a day.

My kindergarten teacher was Miss Neely. She was a nice lady, but all I remember doing in her class was sleeping on a little rug and singing "Postman, postman bring a letter, one for you and one for me." One thing I remember is the variety of classmates. One girl would take red crayon and chew on it. She was cute and quiet, but we had to watch our red crayons.

When I think how we looked to each other, I laugh because I suspect all of us looked strange to each other.

Little did we know we would become very close friends for the next six years and for some of us, for a lifetime. I recall getting off the bus and for weeks staying close to those that got off the bus with us. It did not take long for us to make new friends and become comfortable with them. During those years we were bussed for segregation. Sometimes we passed schools for white students on the way to schools for Black students. I remember one of my friends standing on the corner crying because he couldn't go to school with me. We were neighbors and played together, and separation made no sense to children.

My first grade teacher was Miss Dillon, later Mrs. Boyd. The last time I saw her she was up in age, perhaps close to or more than 90. She remembered me, or at least said she did. My cousin Frank Williams kept up with her over the years. He and I sat with her for more than an hour talking about old times. She must have been a music major because we did an awful lot of singing. It was the first time I learned some basics of group singing. Also, it was my first experience seeing a pitch pipe used.

I enjoyed second grade because at the end of the year I could read almost anything. My sisters discovered me reading portions of their books. They, my brother, and aunt were all excited about my progress. We had spelling words to learn, and my sisters and/or my aunt would go over the words with me each evening. My teacher was Miss Booker, a no-nonsense lady who kept us from recess if we didn't get our work done or needed extra help. I worked hard because I loved recess and did not want to miss running and playing. Neither did Bill Sappington miss recess. Both of us loved running. Secondly, I think most of us studied and listened in Miss Booker's class because this woman, from the very first, put the fear of God in all of us. She was not evil, but her voice and no smile made us think she was. I had a lot of growth in her class, and as I think back, it was this lady that started putting the verbal brick foundation in place for the building that would be erected in the grades to which we were headed. Thank you, Miss Booker, I have not forgotten you.

Art, math, and social cliques come to memory when I look back to third grade. Our teacher was a light-complexioned lady named Miss Campbell. She was good in a number of things, but she must have loved art. She was good at art, and was an above average teacher of art. We had a large cloakroom in those days at the rear of the room. It had a large table which we used to draw and paint, especially finger paint. When we completed our math problems and while waiting for the others to finish, some of us could go to the cloakroom and draw. It did not take us long to see that usually the same students got through first. I am not so sure of our awareness then, but this was the first time cliques were formed. It seems from third grade to sixth grade, this little group of "smart students" hung together for various events. For May Day activities, we did not want a dance partner who was not part of the "cloakroom gang." We had ignorantly formed prejudicial groups based on ability and sometimes on looks.

What a disgrace. There we were - all Black, all poor, all segregated from other ethnic groups, and there we were making differences by a superficial barrier. We were doing to our own what later we would dislike with anger when the larger society did the same to us. To my knowledge that kind of behavior, that foolishness, too often gets by teachers. It took some maturation for us to act on the knowledge that we could be helping the slower students as teachers helped us. Until that maturity came, we were just silly kids — how normal, I don't know.

We did very well in math in third grade also. Miss Campbell was also a good teacher of math.

It seems that all of the progress and readiness from grades kindergarten to three went awry in grade four. The first half of the year we were on a progressive course under an attractive good teacher named Miss Antronette Hall. However, she left, and a substitute came who could not control the few unruly students. After that sub, a permanent teacher named Mrs. Scott came, and for the remaining part of the year, she scared the living daylights out of us, both those who cut up as well as those of us who behaved well. Anyway, under Mrs. Scott we ended the year having experienced some improvement.

The degree to which I want to forget the fourth grade is the same degree to which I want to remember grade five and the teacher, Miss. Cozetta Payne, later Mrs. Kirkland. I loved the ground on which she walked, so to speak. I liked her and the class for at least two good reasons.

First, in her class we learned how to do all kinds of math problems. We received a good amount of instruction in how to do fractions of all kinds. We did extensive work with sentence problems, also called thought problems. I enjoyed her teaching because she showed us why we did certain math operations and what order they were done. She was the first teacher to tell and show us why we did an operation rather than just have us memorize a stepwise process. Equally important to me was her being the first to encourage us to question freely in any area where we genuinely wanted to know something.

Since then, I still ask "why" about things and believe it is in part due to her influence. I recall when I was a preteen, asking a carpenter why he put a level on only two sides of a two by four when he was building a door. He told me that the two by four would be straight up from the floor if you just placed the level on only two sides. I did not understand, and my curiosity was piqued. That "why" question and curiosity was not satisfied until I took plane geometry. There I learned that if a line is perpendicular to two lines in a plane, then it is perpendicular to every line in that plane. Being more mature then and capable of more complex thought, I understood with much excitement. My mind went back to what the carpenter said, and I believe my questioning nature was stimulated by my fifth grade teacher.

Another reason I liked this teacher had little to do with the classroom lesson. It had to do with her character and her perspective on teaching. Miss Payne went beyond the call of duty in my judgment. To put this in perspective, I relate the following incident.

During those years, schools usually had some type of May Day activities. It was an all-day affair with parents invited to see their children perform in some program. Each class had some type of activity to showcase something, either group or individual. It was a high point each year, and we all looked forward to it with high anticipation. For my class activity, the boys needed long white pants. My aunt, on learning of the need, sent a note to Miss Payne saying she did not have the money to purchase pants for me, so I would not be able to participate. Miss Payne sent a written reply in which she stated she would purchase pants for me and that my aunt could pay her when she got the money. I remember well her taking me to J. C. Penney on Minnesota Avenue during the lunch hour and purchasing trousers for me. We went there in the car of my next year's teacher, Miss Lillian Adams, who accompanied us into the store. I participated in the May Day activities. I also took the payment to Miss Payne in two parts. Both notes had thanks included.

In my present thinking, Mrs. Payne was a dedicated teacher, one who went beyond the call of duty. While many teachers did similar things then and now, in those days it was a greater sacrifice and commitment for the Afro-American teacher. The reason was that they received less money contractually than their Caucasian colleagues. Had they not covenanted to such commitment, many of us would not be where we are today. Receiving less financial compensation while giving the same or more service put them in the category of what is often called "Wounded Healers" - that is, while hurting themselves, they labored to heal children in many ways.

After a career of fifty years of teaching I realize that I, too, have made sacrifices. Such sacrifices were partial payment on the debt I owed so many wonderful teachers who were in the mold of Miss Cozetta Payne. I regret that because of being in military service, I did not get a chance to personally say thanks to her again and again. Somehow I have a feeling she knew how much we loved her. Talking with others, I know I am not alone in my feelings about her.

My elementary school years could not have ended with a better team of teachers than those I had in sixth grade. They were two strong, capable teachers. The principal of Grant School, Mr. Daniel Webster Lewis, taught us in the morning. Afternoon sessions were taught by Miss Lillian Adams, who was at Stowe Elementary in the mornings. Both of them spoke English very well. Their verbs and nouns were always in agreement - something from which we could learn. They carried themselves in such a way that if we would emulate their speech and behavior, we would improve. I think Miss Adams could have written an etiquette book, so versed was she in proper behavior.

Mr. Lewis taught us penmanship. How we all remember our dip pens and the inkwell with ink on our desks. Then he taught us how to relax and have correct posture when writing. We learned the proper way to hold a pencil. Then came the ovals and ovals and ovals. We learned the alphabet, both upper and lowercase, using the Palmer technique.

Most of us enjoyed penmanship time, and today most write very well thanks to Mr. Lewis. I took a real liking to writing and lettering because he made it so interesting. I continued writing and have now become an amateur calligrapher, but I learned the basic letter forms in sixth grade from that fine gentleman. I did take time to tell him I appreciated his efforts to pass his knowledge of writing to us. Before he passed, I calligraphed the poem entitled "If" by Rudyard Kipling and gave him a copy. On the bottom I wrote the words "Because of You - Lee Roy." He received it with a big smile and a thank you.

It was Mr. Lewis who led our morning exercise. All grades lined up in the hallway. There we had prayer in unison and recited the American Creed and the Pledge of Allegiance. As I recall, in my sixth grade year we stopped extending our arm to the flag when reciting the pledge of allegiance. He told us that from then on we would just place our hand over our heart. The old way was too much like the Germans did when they said "Heil Hitler."

Quite often he would read some poetry. Often it would be some Black author like Gwendolyn Brooks, Paul Lawrence Dunbar, W.E.B. Dubois, or some other noteworthy writer. He also taught us math. Practically all of our problems that year were thought problems. That meant it required instead of a rote memory process, one that was more analytical in nature. For certain problems, some were called to work on the board. When we were finished we were to squat.

Miss Adams was our afternoon teacher. She taught English and geography, but I recall Mr. Lewis going over some of these also. Sometimes both of them would discuss common learnings such as Civics and the need to be a good citizen. In addition to academics, they were also interested in us knowing the importance of presenting ourselves properly in the best light wherever we would be.

Because I worked hard that year, I really felt like I had learned a lot. I was about twelve years of age. I had been convinced I could learn most anything if I studied. The development of this attitude was in part due to their teaching and motivation.

There were two extracurricular activities that added to my enjoying that year. One was our safety patrol team. Mr. Lewis selected me to be a member of the safety patrol. You had to have good grades and good behavior. Each boy received a badge, shoulder gear, and a yellow raincoat. We were each assigned a street corner where we helped students across the street.

The second activity was something I dearly loved. Each year in Kansas City, Kansas, African American public schools participated in an annual track meet. Each school selected four boys to represent the school in a four by 100 yard relay. The fifth and sixth grades competed while the lower grades had potato races on the football field. It was an all-day affair held at Sumner High School. I made the team both my fifth grade and my sixth grade. I was the only fifth grader on the team when I was in grade five. We looked forward to Field Day, as it was called. Ribbons were given out to winners.

For seven years I was with many of the same students. A few had come from other schools after our first year together, but most had been together for the entire seven years. Regardless of the time together, by grade six we were bonded together in friendships. You could speak a name, and a host of thoughts about that person would come to mind. For the most part, we were comfortable with each other. Those who were physically challenged in some way such as stammering of speech, or those who had difficulty grasping academics and the more gifted, all by then were meshed together. The making fun that we did in lower grades was gone. We had matured greatly. There were still preferences when it came to dance partners or running races, but no making fun of non-dancers. These bonds have remained after many years. We still holler at each other, and given time, we talk about the years past.

Recently I went across town to a church service, and on driving up I thought I knew the security guard out front . Before I got out of the car I realized it was my grade school friend named Herman. My wife went into the service. I started talking with Herman, whom I had not seen in over fifty years. We talked about grade school, classmates, what we'd been doing, our children and family. Before we knew it, church was over.

Then a short time ago, I entered Macedonia Baptist Church for a funeral of a classmate who had been our class president. It was crowded as I entered the vestibule. However, even with all the talk going on, I heard this quiet voice call my name - "Lee Roy, Lee Roy." Just hearing a voice, without looking, I knew it was Marlene Miller (Washington). It had been some forty plus years since I had seen her, but I knew the voice. Such was the bond after seven years together daily for nine months and same teachers. To see Herman and Marlene brought to mind the joys of grade school. The excitement of seeing them and others is an indication of how much I enjoyed my early school years. My Grant School experience, I discovered, was a good foundation for junior high school.

CHAPTER V

REFLECTIONS ON SECONDARY SCHOOL

Secondary school traditionally refers to schooling between primary or elementary and college. We didn't know how much we had been prepared for secondary schooling in the academic sense. I did know I wanted to go, since I had heard my sisters and brother talking about Northeast Junior High School. So now I leave Grant Elementary and head north to Northeast Junior located at Fourth and Troup. Little did I know that on the first day I would see something on the order of 500 to 800 students or more. They were standing on and off the school campus. We were used to seeing much fewer at the schools from which we had come.

It was an exciting, happy experience, but also full of anxiety. I remember looking for someone from Grant School, namely Daniel Jordon, Harry Smith, Dolores, Marlene, Jewell, Ann Graham or any sixth grade friends - to help ease the tension of being new to the place. With the exception of Bill Sappington, none of my other comfort friends were to be found. It was a few minutes before I ran into Bill. We stayed together until we got inside the building. I now wonder how others felt on our first day there.

Now it is fun looking back, but then it was quite an ordeal. Thank God things began to smooth out. There was some anxiety now and then, but nothing that time did not take care of along with personal adjustments and teacher help. Some of us adjusted faster, I am sure, because some had visited the school before then. One classmate lived directly across from Northeast Junior. Then all of us had different levels of biological growth and social maturity. It did not take us boys long to notice far more attractive girls in our classes than at the school from which we came. The girls were not only pretty but were nice and acted like ladies. For a while this was a problem because I found myself thinking about them more than my books. To this day I laugh when I think of the time wasted those first few weeks concentrating on the new girls. Somehow after going to five classes daily, we made new friends and things settled down. I was able to focus on lessons in the presence of teen beauty and classy girls. It was good we got used to it, because those traits were around for the duration of school - and for life.

All of us came from different elementary schools where we knew the principals and they knew each of us by name. Now at Northeast Junior, we had another no-nonsense principal by the name of Joseph Collins. In addition to getting adjusted to him, we also had five new teachers to learn how to please. We had to discover the methods and limits in each class. At first it seemed an impossible task, but soon we had adjusted to this task also. Even before junior high was over, we had grown in ways that caused us to see those teachers in positive ways. Many of them have become significant other persons in our lives in that something they said or did launched us in the right mind set.

The first of many of those teachers was Miss Mattie Williams. She was my seventh grade math teacher, and a good one. One day, along with several others, I received a seventh hour in her class. That meant coming back after school was out. It was uncharacteristic for me to play in class, but for some reason, that day was different. That evening we were to write so many times something like, "I will not talk" or whatever we did wrong. Sometimes she added a touch. With a big smile, she made us write something like "Dear kind, lovable, and adorable Miss Williams, I will not talk in class or chew gum in class" or whatever your "crime" was. In our day those were no-nos. I got through writing before the others, so in childish manner, decided to act out of norm for me. I decided to be funny. It baffles me to this day why I did what I did. I found a safety pin on my clothes and held it up and let it drop. The others saw it and started laughing. What I didn't know was that Miss Williams was looking, though she, with head down, was grading papers. Wise Miss Williams told the other boys to bring their papers up and then they could leave. Then she said, "Pitts, come up here and sit in the desk in front of me." I felt so bad, but the worst was seconds away.

Our teachers in those days could shame us because most of us came from homes where we knew what was correct behavior. After I sat and looked at her, nothing was said for a few minutes. The silence, masterfully used, was killing me. She looked neither angry nor happy, just looked at me looking at her and then elsewhere. I would have been more comfortable had she been angry.

After the long look, she went to work. She said, "Pitts, where are your friends now on this bright sunny evening?" I said, "On their way home." She followed with, "And here you are sitting here looking at my old ugly face." She was not old and far from being ugly. I sat mute with what must have been a stupid look. I wasn't so stupid as to agree with her statement about her looks.

Then came several other questions and statements from her. She asked, "How much do you get paid for acting like a class clown? Do you enjoy being the clown? Pitts, you have a good mind, but here you are wasting it and time." She ended all this by saying, "We will be looking to see how long you plan to keep the job of clown and how long you will waste time and a good mind."

Then while looking at me one more extended time, perhaps a minute, she very slowly and quietly said, "You may go now."

I went out the south door of Northeast Junior High School in a daze. I took my usual left to Third Street and headed home to the West Bottoms. On the way home I felt so low that it seemed that ants on the ground could step on me. I had plenty of time to think about me and what had happened. Before that day I had never played in class and I had never had a seventh hour. After that day I never played in class and never had another seventh hour. Seriousness has been my way of life improvement, thanks to Miss Williams.

At the time I did not know how valuable was the lesson taught and learned as a result of that encounter with a master teacher. She had set things in order so that if I wanted to change, the opportunity could be on my mind. She had helped me stop a behavior that could have become a bad habit. I'll always remember her for that and for being a good math teacher.

Years later, when I went to work at Northeast Junior as a science teacher, Miss Williams was still there. I thanked her for having touched my life in a positive way. It was also my privilege to take her to the doctor a number of times in her late years. One of those times she said, "Pitts, I think you like me."

I said, "No, I love you." I told her about the incident that occurred some twelve to fifteen years before. She did not recall it, but said that sounded like her. Both of us laughed. Then with seriousness of purpose, I told her I thought she was a beautiful Black woman who knew how to motivate young people. She thanked me and asked how my oldest sister and brother were doing. She had taught all five of us and knew us by name. Such was the value of neighborhood schools. Miss Williams had a wonderful sense of humor and so we laughed when I told her I hoped she didn't mess all of us up. While both of us smiled, she said, "I hope not."

Later, she was Mrs. Commodore. I still smile when I think about this lady who greatly affected me.

One of the high points of junior high school was taking physical education. In the seventh grade I could hardly wait for eighth grade to start P.E., as it was called. Then when it came, I could hardly wait for the hour I was to be in the gym. That was the year I met another no-nonsense teacher. "Another" is applicable because in grade seven I had two such male teachers and three female.

Our P.E. teacher was Mr. Harold Wright, who was dressed in white on gym days. Gym was every other day. On non-gym days, we had health class from him. On those days he was dressed as usual in suit and tie. Mr. Wright in all that I knew then and years later, was a gentleman in every sense of the term. I think all boys loved P.E. because it was our first time learning about using apparatus like parallel bars, the horse, rope climbing, and tumbling. We got a chance to run, play basketball, softball outdoors and have lots of action. As I stated, I do not recall any boys not enjoying gym. Most hated when Mr. Wright blew the whistle indicating time to go to the showers.

Little did I know that many things about the body that I learned in health I would see later in more complex biology courses. So in a couple later classes, a number of things looked familiar.

As was the case with all of my teachers at Northeast Junior High School, I never heard foul language or cursing come from Mr. Wright. He also had a way of making you believe he cared, even when he was getting on your case for something you did wrong. Over the years my respect grew for this fine man. Later when I went to work at Northeast, I lived only two blocks from him. By then my oldest sons, Lee and Eric, had also been in his class and had the same respect for him as I did. My two youngest children didn't have the opportunity to be in his class, but they did get to meet him.. Of course, my wife knew him when she was a student at Northeast. He always asked me, "How is the madam?" referring to my wife, and he'd ask, "How is your daughter?"

I kept in touch with him. When he got so he couldn't drive, I took him to St. Louis to visit his sister. Our son Eric's medical practice was in St. Louis, and Mr. Wright beamed with delight when he learned that Eric was a medical doctor.

After a career of fifty years of teaching and having done the research, I know something about my teachers. I know we were fortunate to have had a cadre of men at Northeast who academically could hold their own in any school system then and now. The male teachers I had were superb, and a few come to mind. Mr. Webster McGee - Industrial Arts; Mr. Clarence Glasse - Mathematics; Mr. Glasco - Mathematics; Mr. Donald Boone - Industrial Arts; Mr. William Boone - Science; Mr. Bertram Caruthers - Science; and Mr. Richard Warren - Mathematics.

And all of these teachers had their unique way of relating to and getting the attention of students. You would act up with a few, and a very few. If you were a student who liked to act up, be unruly, disruptive, or just plain out of control, you would only do it one time in most of these gentlemen's classes. They would take care of you, and it would not be child abuse. They would not allow students to interfere with the education process going on in their classes. Each had their own way of putting a stop to foolishness, and some were good at stopping it before it got started.

One day I saw Mr. McGee stop class and ask a boy who was being disruptive, "Son, are you having a problem that you want me to solve?" Now Mr. McGee was a man with little fat and could look at you with a stare that would indicate he could take care of things. A sensible boy would get the message. Mr. McGee had the strength to pick up a good-size boy and place him on the bench in our woodworking class. Because he kept order, we learned much and accomplished much in projects. I never knew any boy that did not like Mr. McGee.

Then there was a teacher I had for freshmen math named Mr. Clarence Glasse. He was a handsome man with a Clark Gable-type mustache. When we acted up in his class, he would simply say, "Boy, come here," and it would not be very loud. He might have a big smile on his face with a hand gently on your shoulder, but you knew he meant business when he suggested that he would take care of you and your business if you wouldn't. Then with seriousness he would ask you, "Are you going to take care of your business?" All of us liked Mr. Glasse because he was a good math teacher.

Equal to my love for P.E. and math was my love for my first year of science. Mr. Bertram Caruthers was the teacher.

Like Mr. Glasse, he was handsome and brown skinned. Seldom were there disruptions in his class other than a few boys getting too loud in the back of the room. To this he would say something like "You birds back there may stay, but that noise has to go." If things continued, which it seldom did, he might ask, "Do you want me to come back there with my board?" More often he would be diplomatic, saying to an individual, "We can't let you disturb the good that's going on in our class." This teacher had the gift of making you feel like he thought you were number one. He was very personable and as such, I think everyone liked him. Because he did a lot of demonstrations, he made the subject interesting. I never wanted to be late to his class, I loved it so.

Mr. Caruthers was the first and only teacher to visit my home on my behalf. I well remember how nervous I was to learn that he was knocking on our door. It was dinnertime ("supper," as we called it). My aunt always asked visitors if they would like some supper. We had a large round table that sat in the middle of the room. I was nervous at first, but later felt some better as he spoke about me to my aunt. For a while it was something like a daze. Here was a teacher, my teacher, who cared enough to come across the bridge, down James Street, past two slaughterhouses, one scrap iron company, and knock on the door of the little three-room shotgun house at 9 North Second Street. I say this because as I sat there, momentarily I thought of how many people did not like to come down to the Bottoms. Before he said anything, I wondered why he came because I never did anything wrong in classes.

It was in his class that I first began to understand the futility and nonsense of believing in superstitions. Being raised by older, uneducated aunt and uncle, superstitions were almost a daily thing. One assignment we had was to bring in five or so superstitions. I recall that I had enough to give to anyone who was shy of the number needed. Before this class, unlike my sister Mat, I never believed very much in superstitions because my Uncle Alf had said there was nothing to them. However, whatever ones I was tempted to belicve were put to rest during my sojourn for a year with Mr. Bertram Caruthers. He later became Dr. Caruthers. It was in his class that I first heard about the scientific method, BTUs, horsepower, and stories of the works of pioneer scientists like Alexander Graham Bell. I enjoyed reading our textbook so much that I could hardly put it down. I read it when often I should have been studying other books.

I do not remember doing a lot of talking in his class, but I remember listening to him and watching him. As I said, he often did demonstrations using a Bunsen burner and other equipment. It was all new to us and usually we sat spellbound. Very early I noticed that he had a way of answering you, though your inquiry was wrong or off key, to make you feel important and never put down. Especially was that important to me because of some things going on in my life at the time.

Little did I know how much one year of basic general science would benefit me later in higher science courses. It was not so much the facts learned as the philosophy and methodology that was so useful and fascinating to me. Since then I have had many good teachers, but none better.

Of all my teachers from elementary to high school, I had a negative opinion of only one. It was my seventh grade woodworking teacher. I thought Mr. Wade was a lazy one who did not know how to handle boys. As I look back now, I still believe he should not have hung out the title "teacher" on a shingle. Other than him, I thought I had good teachers who were not only gifted in their craft but also taught students their subject. Always we were first in their minds. They showed that they cared in many other ways.

As an example of such caring spirit, I relate this incident. It was my seventh grade. I had noticed the neat dress of the teacher, Mr. Donald Boone. I was to be in his metalwork class for half a year. It was now about three weeks to a month into this semester. I went to him after school by myself and asked him if he would show me how to tie the type of knot that he wore in his tie. He asked me if I had a tie, to which I said, "No, sir." He then removed his tie and with me watching him, he tied what I learned was a Windsor knot. He then stood behind me, and he placed it around my neck and, being much taller, proceeded to lean over me and slowly step by step tie that tie. Then while looking down at me, he let me tie it several times until I did so without help. Then he showed me how to put the dimple in the center of the tie. He told me the name of the knot and the history. Last, he placed the tie in my hands and said, "You may have it." He had a big smile as I said, "Thank you, Mr. Boone." I think he knew how surprised and happy I was at that moment.

I left Northeast by way of the south side, and, as always when I did not leave with Sugarman, took the left to Third Street. I took a right on Third Street and headed home. On the way home I must have stopped a million times to tie my tie. Mr. Boone taught Industrial Arts, but he went beyond the subject. He gave me a tie, true enough, but to me at that age he gave me the most important thing, and that was to care enough to show it. He put into my head and hands that "know how." He saw in me the will or guts to come, and he learned that I did not know the way. He, like so many of our teachers back then, became my way - my hope. So today I wear a Windsor knot most of the time, not to remember the Duke of Windsor, but to remember an Afro American male teacher who was concerned enough to go the extra mile. That teacher was Mr. Donald Boone.

So much more could be said about our teachers and the era that impacted my life. I will take time to speak of only one other. This was my freshman English teacher. She was a tall lady who spoke elegantly and in addition to being well versed in English, was one of the kindest teachers. We were respectful of her but not tense or afraid in her presence. She was Miss Etta Mae Jackson. Recently I learned of her location and have written to and received correspondence from her. I had an opportunity to speak with her; she is nearing 90. She resides in Tucson, Arizona, with her husband, Mr. Sidney Dawson.

What was so special about this lady that I would remember her over the many years? It was a combination of her personality, what she taught, and how she taught it. In her class we learned the importance and application of parts of speech and correct usage. We had learned some of this before, but not at the level we learned in her class. Then I recall that we learned much new material, such as diagramming sentences to better understand parts of speech. Somehow, for some reason, all of that was very meaningful to me.

She stressed the importance of topics in such a way that I started trying to practice in my talk what we learned in class. I tried to improve my writing and speech not so much for a grade, but because I saw the benefits. Her personality also was the kind that made you feel important and therefore I never wanted to miss her class. To me her class drew my attention as much as science class and physical education, and that's saying a lot.

A few years ago we had our fiftieth year high school reunion, and as with all reunions, teacher talk became a part of an evening. In speaking about our teachers, Miss Jackson's name was mentioned. One classmate who was in Miss Jackson's class with me leaned over and said, "Good, better, best." Then she asked if that brought back any memories. With surprised smiles, we looked at each other and recited the following which we learned in her class:

Good, better, best
Never let it rest
Until your good is better
And your better is best.

That was Miss Etta Mae Jackson in brief. She made us thirsty in the areas of writing and speaking. By far I am not where I would like to be, nor was English my emphasis in college. However, I knew the contribution of Miss Jackson was a push in the right direction for me.

It is interesting how after fifty years I became reconnected to this fine lady. The wife of one of my classmates heard me speak highly of Miss Jackson and said she knew where she was and had her address. Dorothy McField, wife of my longtime friend, James McField, gave me her address, and I corresponded with her. To my surprise, I learned that Miss Jackson is also a graduate of Sumner High School, 1936 class. I know two of her classmates. One was Miss Josephine Campbell, later Mrs. Josephine Vandiver Boone; and another was Mrs. Alice Curry Penn. I saw a picture of their graduating class, and many of them are well known persons who have and still are making significant contributions to our community. We were influenced by many like-minded and character building people.

The year before last, 2007, I had not received a response from Miss Jackson for a while. Our daughter, Gina, went to a meeting of her sorority, Alpha Kappa Alpha, in Arizona. Knowing I was trying to make contact with Miss Jackson, she inquired about her among her members. With much joy she called me with information on how to make contact with her. I did so, and am now back in touch. I gave her an update on our city development as well as our classmates. Her mind is still sharp, though she said she is having to get used to others helping her.

There were some other teachers who, though I did not have a class with them, outside of class were helpful in some way. Had I been in their presence longer, I would have avoided many mistakes. However, due to no fault of any teacher, my high school years were short lived because of two reasons that will be explained more fully in another chapter.

I chose to elaborate on the above-mentioned teachers because they impressed and had an effect on my thinking at a crucial time during my developmental teen years. The older members of my family were all extremely good thinkers, but the ones around me had less to offer me academically. Therefore because of hearing new views I took very early to listening to my teachers and the opportunity that school provided. For years now I have tried to pay tribute to my teachers by keeping their memories alive. I have done so when I have given seminars, lectures, and graduation speeches.

CHAPTER VI

MY SOCIAL DEVELOPMENT AND ACTIVITIES

All teenagers are going to develop physically, psychologically, and emotionally. The degree of normalcy in these areas is determined a lot by the environment and social life of a teen. I grew up in a segregated environment, so many of the things afforded other races and ethnic groups were not available to me or my peers. Some social interactions with other races were not ours to experience. My interactions were greater than many because the West Bottoms had many ethnic groups. However, even there we saw a selective segregation. Some economically poor whites still acted as if they were superior to minorities. We never played basketball or football or ran track against any school that was for white children. Our only experience competing against whites was at the Kansas University Relays held annually in April.

As Black youth, we had the same social needs as others. We had the same kinds of stresses to overcome as others. We were typical teens, with typical wants over and above needs. More than anything, we needed assistance in understanding our own growth needs. As is so often the case with poor people as we were, my folks were not equipped to give quality guidance as professional teachers or preachers. So for me, the good teachers I had along with the environment of some classes and outside school activities went a long way to help my development. Most of my unbearable things were outside of the school.

It did not take long to learn that I was not alone in not having many of my needs and wants fulfilled. My folks had drilled into us the need to make do with what you have in order to survive and succeed. However, that is easier said than done for a youngster. I found it easier to accept that "make do" philosophy in elementary school than in junior high and above. So to help us through the teens, our parents, teachers, and a few community organizations provided some activities to help us have a proper focus while we learned to handle our social, psychological, and physical development.

One such activity that meant much to me was intramural basketball. This took place before classes each morning during the fall semester in junior high school. It allowed a number of boys who were not on the school team to "show off" or improve in basketball. Each home room selected a team, and homeroom teams played other homerooms. Naturally, the girls and other students came early to see the games and holler yells for their team. As simple as it may seem, this activity fulfilled both a physical need and a social development need, since it enhanced our self esteem. In my case, it helped me feel good to hear some girls say, "You play good" or "You have big legs." It helped me cope with some of the not-so-good things that were occurring at home. My circle of friends widened, and I felt good because I got a chance to show that I could do something.

Years later, after working at Northeast, I learned that the "brain" that originated the intramural idea was our gym teacher, Mr. Harold Wright. It is an example of how our teachers were looking out for us in many ways. They did not brag about it but showed it by their actions.

Another activity that I enjoyed was track and field. I excelled in the sprints and was a member of the 4 by 100 relay team in my freshman year. I watched James Madison, Charles Harlan, and Vernon Coffee for a couple years as they ran the hurdles, before I got to high school. I was certain I could run the low hurdles and use my speed between hurdles to compensate for deficiency of form. Madison and Harlan taught me how to hurdle. All of those fellows were upperclassmen at Sumner High School. They were an inspiration to us; we always looked forward to going there to replace them. I won a school letter on the varsity track team.

These extracurricular programs were of school origin, but there were programs that were co-sponsored by school and some community organizations. The goal was the same with them all, namely to add to our social development and the advancement of our academic progress. Speaking about the involvement of outside agencies for helping students, two come to mind. I recall hearing about the "High-Y" for boys and the "Y Teens" for girls. The Black component of the YWCA was located at Seventh and Quindaro. It was run by Miss Gladys Burke and Miss Powell. The Y-Teens was a social outlet where girls learned social graces, dancing, hiking, or bowling. A classmate, Dolores Pierce Elliott, related this to me. She said she enjoyed the Y Teens. She also spoke of a few other social clubs to help teens. The High-Y was similar in function but for boys. Both of these were co-sponsored by the YMCA and the YWCA.

Another very exciting event sponsored by the Yates branch of the Y was "Teen Town." It was an activity only for teens and took place on Friday evenings. The purpose was again to cultivate the social graces of associating with our peers. Dances and other group activities were held. Mrs. Dorothy McField, wife of my classmate, James McField, spoke with me about the high excitement of Teen Town. Just speaking with her about it made me regret not being in on that event. All of this was segregated, of course, due to the times in society.

I knew about some of these useful activities but never got to participate because most of these convened after school. Normally I had to go home immediately after school to complete chores. I was seldom able to participate in any event that was regularly scheduled after school. I was not alone in missing out on these organizational activities. Students who lived in Rosedale, Armourdale, and Argentine had trouble being involved with things after school because they rode a bus to and from school. If they missed the bus, they would have to ride public transit. I lived some distance from schools, and so in grade school a bus was provided from and to the West Bottoms. However, when we got to Northeast Junior and Sumner High, we had to walk both ways.

What this meant in effect was that while a number of good activities were in place, they were yet not accessible to all of us. It was beneficial to live near the schools. Generally, this meant living between Third Street on the east to about Twelfth Street on the west, Quindaro on the north, and Minnesota on the south. These boundaries were irregular but they were, generally speaking, our "hood." The Bottoms, Rosedale, Armourdale, and Argentine were also extended hoods.

Our teachers, community leaders, and parents worked to stabilize our lives then, but they were also thinking of our future. It would be a while after teen life that I would understand growth changes on the way to becoming a man. I am so glad that many of our teachers were working with our parents to help us experience certain events and to avoid unhelpful events. Many of the activities they planned were to keep us on track for future success. I later learned that every child needs adults in their life to guide them through turbulent waters.

Speaking of socializing, life in the seventh grade found me liking two or more girls. I made friends with two or more boys also who had not been at Grant School with me. So early in grades seven, my circle of friends began to grow. Most of the time, I liked the girls because of the way they looked outwardly. The boys I became friends with were usually quiet and serious in class, as was I. This was probably true for all my classes except gym class, where we were all usually excited and noisy. It is interesting after fifty plus years to ask classmates how they perceived me at that time in our lives. I have received at least several variations on a theme, all positive. I think many, if not most of us, had a mix of feelings as we started our social intercourse with the opposite sex.

By the time I was in my freshman year, I was socially more mature. I recall how near the latter part of grade eight into the ninth grade, much growth took place in every way, and I felt more secure within myself. One notable change was I began to see something in girls other than just physical build. I always enjoyed girls who were clean, neat, and smart, but not boisterous. It then seemed that these and other intrinsic character traits were even more important to me. At least I was now more aware and focused on character.

In grade eight I first noticed a certain girl for all the things I liked in girls. I was seeing her in several classes. She was one of the most intelligent students in class and seemed to have it all: speech, carriage, appropriate dress, and relating well with others. I got enough courage to let her know that I wanted to talk to her after school. At first she was smart enough to stay close to a girlfriend after school when she knew I was interested in seeing her alone. I was persistent enough that by the end of the eighth grade we were talking regularly, and I was walking her home. I knew if I got home late, trouble would be waiting for me, but by then it was worth it, says the teen hormones.

By the ninth grade I was often walking her home after school. I met her grandmother and grandfather and afterwards on Saturday walked the Avenue with her quite often. She was my first girlfriend, and she said I was her first boyfriend, as we called it during our times. For me and for her, this was big time. She discovered my positives and I discovered that all that I thought I saw in her, she really possessed. I teased her about being a track star since she walked so fast.

I spoke of her grandmother and grandfather. She never used those terms when referring to them. Rather she wanted me to meet her "Big Daddy" and her "Mother Dear." In the language of my upbringing, Black family life, it meant grandfather and grandmother. Southern families, Black and white, use the same idiom with fondness.

During those mid-teens many, if not most of us, just wanted relations with a nice person of the opposite sex, since we already had a number of close friends of our own sex. Little did we know about the development phases of youth, but we were most surely going through them. How I recall in college psychology class learning about such phases when studying "Havighurst Developmental Tasks" of people.

Bill Sappington and I walked all over town going to see or meet girls that we liked or wanted to get to know better. It is good that at ages twelve to mid-teens the good Lord grants much energy and a short recovery time. How else could we waste so much time and recover enough to get some work done at home as well as endure the scolding for not being on time?

In any event, some of the girls we met became good friends, and some of those friendships have lasted for many years. When we returned from military service, some of our once close friends were married with children. Some of these friendships led to new friends. We met two sisters, Ervine and Jewell Holmes, who lived in Missouri. They often came to the Bottoms to visit their uncle. They lived next door to a boy that I later worked with - Earl Grant. Seeking relationships with girls was both good and bad, depending on the perspective. Regardless, one could learn from those years.

We are all adults now looking back at those growing pains, joy and regrets, and are able to laugh as we put things into proper perspective. Recently I became reacquainted with the girl with whom I was so enamored during junior high and early high school. We talked freely about those years and our relationship in particular. We acknowledged what we did not know back then or would not accept. Namely, life's truths, that sometimes Gloria likes George but George likes Sandra. Sandra is hoping John will check her out. Also many of us then didn't know how to respond or communicate our real feelings. Often that is life experience and perhaps more so during our teen years.

For some of us the teen years were fun, for some a nightmare. We missed all kinds of cues that would have lessened some hurts or increased some joys. Yes, we missed cues from girls, boys, parents, and teachers, but more important we missed, too often, life's lessons. The lesson was learning and accepting that all of our wants will not be fulfilled; nor are they necessarily what is best for us. I learned this lesson earlier than I could accept emotionally. However, when I saw it, understood and accepted it, I knew much growth had taken place.

Much of our experience back then causes us to laugh in our senior years. For example, when I remember how in seventh grade I wondered where all those pretty girls had come from, to my later feelings of being in love with five of them at the same time, I now laugh. When I spoke about that time with Bill Sappington, he said he was in love with twenty or so girls that year. I laughed more. Then I reflect on all the wasted time we spent going to visit girls whose mothers often would not let us on the porch to see their daughter. I suppose we looked like little vagabonds as we stood on the sidewalk, in the street, or in their yard with our jeans and t-shirts that showed our muscles. The mothers should have known we were ready to climb up and get the moon for their daughters. All of the immaturity and thinking we were on top of it brings so much laughter now we can hardly stop.

We look back and see that in one sense we were silly boys lucky to get out of the teens with character and focus. Was my life during those years typical of many, if not most boys in regard to girls? Often I have asked myself that question. I think, minus this or that, for the most part, my journey was normal. Most of us boys were trying to fit in, and to do so we did whatever was necessary to accomplish that goal. Some faked coolness in some way, some lied to other boys about their supposed successes, and some were wiser and focused correctly on proper balance of books and girls.

Such balance was certainly enhanced if and where one's home environment gave guidance and other advantages.

Thank goodness in spite of it all we made it through those years and others to follow. A number of people can be credited for assisting me: my Aunt Lydia, my Uncle Alfred, and my teachers who made school a haven. I grew because of the fun and trials of the journey.

Our years at Northeast Junior High School were capped off with graduation at the Memorial Hall. Though we graduated in a robe, my aunt wanted me to have a nice pair of pants for the affair. We went to the dry goods store at Central and James Street called Traxler's to get the pants. The only thing they had in my size was pants of a tuxedo. The entire suit was not much more than the pants, since it was a used tuxedo. Inasmuch as we often received hand-me-down clothes from the Traxler family, and also their store sold new and used clothes, I am sure one way or the other, the Traxlers were the source of my tuxedo. My aunt worked at the Traxlers' home which was away from the Bottoms. Regardless of where they came from, at least I had new pants for graduation.

I had been selected by Miss Caldwell and Miss Williams as a commencement speaker. However, I could not stay after school and so was not a speaker in the end. So there I was sitting at graduation with a tux when I would rather have been speaking to my classmates in jeans or overalls under the robe. I never told anyone about having been selected, but one of my classmates, Wilma Robertson, remembered I was selected and told someone, because at our recent fiftieth reunion, several people remarked that I could have been one of the speakers.

That night may not have been the way it could have been or the way I wanted, but it did not stop me from enjoying the evening. The important thing was that I graduated and was headed to Sumner High School. The next day, and off and on during that summer we went to Swope Park to extend our moment of joy. Sometimes we went with some family member or several of us would get together and go. It was a time of excitement for adults as well.

The Black church was another positive for us in the summers. Many good size churches would have picnics. Even when your folks were not a member, often friends or family members of the church would invite you. Folks ate and participated like family in memorable activities like horseshoes, playing ball or catch, walking a girl to the zoo, and swinging. We teen boys delighted in seeing how high we could swing the girls. They would scream more, the higher we went. Sometimes we knew some were not afraid, but most of the time their screams fed our egos. We were usually dressed in jeans and t shirts, flexing our muscles.

There was no place to swim at Swope Park. All of these activities were usually on a hill near the zoo at Shelter Number Five. Though we were limited in where we could go in the park and the city, we were not limited in the fun we had as children. As young preteens and early teens, we were so aware of the joys of life that stresses were not so apparent. However, as we took on more responsibility, so stress increased.

CHAPTER VII

TROUBLE IN THE WAY STATION

Going to live with our Aunt Lydia was analogous to going to a way station. A way station is a stop off place between where you were and the destination to which you are heading. This analogy perspective was not what I held in my youth and early adulthood. However, what occurred while living with Aunt Lydia fits extremely well with a few way stations I experienced in the military. Some problems in those stations were a natural consequence of the number of men being held, the tension erupting due to crowding, and the varying mindsets of the men involved. Often I saw problems because of the lack of skills on the part of the leaders to influence and or control us soldiers.

In this chapter I am going to share the problems that surfaced and some of the consequences of those problems. As much as I can recall, I will tell it with the view and feelings of my living it at that time. Near the end of the chapter I will attempt to share a later perspective on all that occurred during the time covered. It is important to remember that in my youthful days I was not experiencing my problems with the way station analogy in mind.

When most of us are very young we are experiencing so much joy that stress is limited in scope or not noticed as much. Around the sixth or seventh grade I became aware of stress in our home. However, at first I had little anxiety about it. Mainly, I wasn't worried about what would happen because I was yet around others whose responsibility was to oversee us younger ones.

From the sixth grade to the ninth, things at home were rough for me. School really was the best of times for me because classes and fun with a few friends served as a buffer to a few not-so-right happenings at home.

My worst of times actually began around 1945. My older brother, Albert Rice, was killed in the United States Navy. He was aboard the USS Indianapolis, a heavy cruiser that took part of the atomic bomb to the island of Tinian. The ship was torpedoed and went down July 30, 1945, at fifteen minutes after midnight. For me, more than a ship went down. Albert had just turned twenty the 11th of June, and I had just had my thirteenth birthday that 11th of May. He had been the most influential family member in my life before and after our mother died. So a part of my fun, encouragement, and other experience went down with that ship.

My brother's nickname was Bud. Bud was a good brother not only to me but also to his twin Alberta and our other two sisters, Evelyn and Madeline.

To better understand what I was to experience after my brother's loss, one needs to have knowledge of our home environment before he left. It must be remembered that a decision was made that was in our best interest. It was decided that Aunt Lydia would take us. She had no children and her taking us would keep us together. Inasmuch as the alternatives were going separately to other family members or all of us going to an orphanage, Aunt Lydia being willing and able to take all five of us was nothing short of an unexpected encounter with Grace. My uncle, Isom Love, was not present, but I am sure that he consented to the decision.

Years later, there would be reasons to wonder if he had consented to the decision.

For the two of them never to have had children and then suddenly have five must have been very stressful. We were experiencing stress also, especially Mat, Alberta, and Bud, because of their greater awareness. All of us had just had a detachment from our mother. So with the best environment, we had some adjustment and understanding to do. Looking back, I can see how the skills of a professional social worker could have made the transition smoother for both children and surrogate parents. All this was during the Great Depression of the 1930s, so the economic times alone would be stressful for a two-child family, not to mention a new five-child family.

We were used to spending short periods at Aunt Lydia's, but never overnight or all day. With the exception of having old views for raising children and believing children should be seen and not heard, Aunt Lydia was good. She was and still remains one of the cherished persons in my life. She was strong willed and could take care of herself in most situations. She was a good and deep thinker. She was born in 1893 in a rural setting in Kaw Valley. Her father, Thomas Lockridge, taught all of the children how to survive in that setting. I know nothing of which she or her siblings were afraid, man or beast. She was compassionate, helpful to people, and loved to talk. She was the neighborhood counselor to adult women who were having husband troubles.

My uncle also was fearless, but sociable and outgoing only to people he already knew. His background was rural Tennessee as a youngster, and he, also, had lost his mother early in life. His work at the metal works company in the Bottoms, I. J. Cohen, was hard and dangerous. Yet unless he was sick or injured, he went to work every day. I never recall feeling insecure or afraid of outside persons while living at home. As I grew older, my main problem was finding peace with my uncle's beliefs about children and work. His weakness of weekend alcohol sprees was a hindrance.

He believed that if someone was feeding you and putting a roof over your head, then all children needed was to work 24/7, minus sleep. So from the beginning at 10 Ohio Street, my older brother and sister had problems when he didn't want either of them to go around the corner to play or even to Uncle Alfred's. It was not a case of disobedient children or children not knowing the proper way to respond to adult requirements. Nor do I think it was parent figures who were deliberately trying to make life hard for children.

Again, as I look back, I believe so much good could have come to all of us had we been exposed to a social worker who was looking out for the children. I do recall a social worker coming to our home before my older brother and sister left home. It was a Miss Smith. Never did she speak to or question the children, not even my brother and sister. In my opinion, this was a failure of the system. Without such help, the next thing that happened was inevitable.

As time went on, we got older and the problem was exacerbated. As long as Alberta and Albert were home, they became shields for us younger ones. Whenever any of us children asked questions for any reason, my uncle could get very angry and unreasonable. Things would escalate when Alberta would try to explain her side or Mat's and my side. Alberta talked fast and even as a mid-teenager, her logic and rational thought was as one older. So I was told by my older cousin Emmett Lockridge. I was too young to know anything about logic, but I did know at eight years of age what made sense and what seemed fair. She and Bud would tell Madeline and me to be quiet, and so we were covered by them from hurts or trouble that could have been caused by our wrongful speech. My sister Mat seldom got in trouble later because of words because she had a soft, quiet demeanor about her. She could take a lot of wrong without retaliating. That was something that was not my strength even when I was young, and it did not get better as a teenager. My sister Evelyn was always better off because she was always treated as the baby.

Often during heated friction with our uncle, Bud would tell me to come along with him. We would go outdoors to either clean the yard or cut wood. At 10 Ohio Street we had a large garage where the ceiling was high enough to swing an axe or saw wood. He used to talk to me out there, and sometimes we played marbles since the floor was dirt.

Alberta from early on always looked after Mat when the fussing started. My older sister and brother seemed to know that we had nowhere else to go since all the other aunts and uncles were not accessible. Uncle Tommy (my mother's brother, Thomas Lockridge) was out of the city and unmarried.

As I stated in an earlier chapter, while stress mounted, not only did I have my sister and brother, but school was a relief from home problems. When I was ten years of age, my brother and sister left home, one year before Albert was eighteen and drafted. When he was home he was responsible for the outside work and since I was five I helped. Long before he left I had learned from him how to handle an axe and the two types of saws we used. He had shown me how to avoid accidents when cutting difficult pieces of wood like crossties and wood with many knots. I had gotten experience at home and over at Uncle Alf's house. I was only ten when he left, but stronger than most 10 year olds. I could cut or saw any kind of wood.

After my brother left, I was responsible for all outside work. I had to find wood to cut sometimes. After cutting it, I brought some in and stacked it in the wood box behind the stove and some on the back porch. At 24 North Second we had chickens, and later at 9 North Second we had both chickens and hogs. Then I had to locate wood and cut and stack it along with feeding the livestock. I kept both the areas clean and at times put lime in the chicken coops or other insect repellant. Additionally, I was the one who went to the store with my aunt to bring home flour and whatever was heavy.

My sister Madeline always felt sorry for me seldom having time to play and so would come out to help me cut wood. She thought she could help me get free time to play. She was awkward at cutting wood and was scared to put her foot on the wood, so when she cut she would scatter wood and make more work. I liked my sister and did not like to see her do that kind of work. But she was helpful in some small way.

Bud was working at the packinghouse and living elsewhere for one year before being drafted. Sometimes he would come by when my uncle was not home and help me as much as possible or see how I was doing. Mostly he was available for me to share my feelings.

When we were at 24 North Second Street, we had inside water. Then we supposedly moved up in the world when my uncle purchased two houses. There was no electricity or water in either house. So another chore was added to my list of responsibilities. I now had to "pack water" from the feed store for our inside use. We needed water for five people since Bud and Bert were gone. We needed water to feed the hogs. Then washday - which came once a week - for me was a nightmare. Before going to school in the morning I had to fill a tub on the stove and another with water. There was wash water, rinse water, and some water called bluing water. In the evening I had to empty water that Aunt Lydia had not emptied. Some washdays I stayed home just to pack water.

I was never afraid of hard work. I was aware that because of the work, I was better developed and stronger than many boys my age. Work was not my problem. The problem was I had no time to participate in anything after school or in the neighborhood. Even when I would cut enough wood to last several days, I was to be home in case I was needed. I had a couple of friends, Bill and Rufus, who also had some physically taxing chores, but neither of them spent as much time working as I did. They could at least have a modicum of normal growing up. For example, by the time we were nearing thirteen years, I would occasionally see a number of friends playing baseball on Cooper School ground. It was the campus of a school that had been torn down, but the vacant field was in use by young people. I missed participating in those kinds of games.

When I became aware of opportunities after school and the limited social activities in the Bottoms, knowing I could not be involved left me a not-so-happy young person, to say the least. I often had frequent hopeful thoughts of things improving, but it seems they didn't, so I ran away around twelve years of age. I went to visit my daddy, only to discover he could not keep me. After that, I often had fleeting thoughts of how I could get away from it all. The most uncomfortable of my thoughts was the thought of being away from my two sisters who were there with me still. It was especially uncomfortable to think of being away from our baby sister, Evelyn. Since kindergarten I had always looked after her because we were together at the same grade school while Madeline was at Stowe Elementary School and my older brother and sister were at Northeast Junior or Sumner. Then Madeline always seemed stronger than Evelyn. During her early grade school years, Evelyn was very shy. Life's struggles changed all of that. As she approached her middle to late teens, Evelyn was much more forthright and frank.

By the time I was in the ninth grade, I was still an unhappy youngster at home. At school I was by then able to mask my feelings enough to still get my lessons. Now having made friends and having won the interest of a very special girl also kept my interest in school high and was a balm for the hurtful feelings I had about home. My attitude and view of home were both real and perceived. I felt like some of my upset times were provoked because I believed no one was thinking of my needs even when I was doing more work than normally required of others my age.

To compound my problem, at the time I had lost two people from my daily environment who were good sounding boards for me. My favorite uncle, Alfred Lockridge, had passed. Then my closest childhood and teen friend, Bill, in our eighth grade, moved across the river to live with his mother and his brothers and sisters. It left me walking to and from school by myself, three and a half miles each way. A walk that had been shared by the two of us was now a lonely road.

He had been living with his grandmother, Mrs. Lucille Smith, since kindergarten. His moving was a first for us, because since early grade school we had talked every day and thereby handled any problems either of us were going through at home or at school. I can't think of much that we didn't talk about, as boys do and need. Naturally, during our developmental period, girls were one of our main subjects.

He knew who I liked, and I knew who he liked. Our friendship certainly was meaningful to me and went far in helping me cope with my home environment.

After he moved, other families with children also moved. By the eighth grade I remember only two other young people living on the Kansas side of Kaw Valley. When I headed to Northeast Junior and later Sumner, I walked by myself. When something came up at home, I would just walk away and head for Bill's. Heading for his house near Fourth and Oakland, I usually had a mind to spend whatever time I wanted and take whatever consequences when I returned home. Since my uncle believed children and young people had no need for anything other than work, my extended stay only exacerbated the negative vibes between us. But I learned that being away from home was good for me.

The last few weeks of the ninth grade a friend named Leroy Green told me about a job as a busboy at Hotel Muehlbach Coffee Shop on Twelfth Street in Kansas City, Missouri. We both went to work there, and during those few weeks that we were still in school, we worked from 11:00 p.m. to 7:00 a.m. I bought some pants, a shirt, and a sweater for myself, then gave the rest of the money to my aunt for my sisters. I still had to do my chores, but I noticed that they were more lenient when I was working. I was also more tired, but I did not sleep in classes those two weeks.

We worked there through the summer before going to Sumner High. We had a good coffee shop manager named Don. He tried to work as many young school guys as possible. He thought we were in high school. He knew I wanted to be moved to the three to 11:00 p.m. shift, which would have enabled me to continue to work when at Sumner. However, that time was already taken by other boys who had been there longer. One such boy was Earl Grant, then a student at Lincoln High School in Kansas City, Missouri. Earl was already an accomplished musician and vocalist. He went on to become nationally known, but remained a good friend until his death. Leroy became a well known professional boxer.

The work at the coffee shop was good for me and our family. One time my uncle got hurt on the job, and the money I brought home helped very much. He also fussed less when I brought money home. So the work was a hedge between me and my uncle when and if he was not in a good mood.

Later in life, I would learn that many of my classmates also encountered impediments of sorts that differed from an ideal environment. Some experienced problems of family disconnections as did I. Then all of us felt the negatives brought on by being poor.

In spite of impediments, I still received enough positive experiences from school to have had a successful school year. I was still internally motivated to want to continue on to Sumner High School. This was something we just had from grade school days. We would say, "All I want to be is a Spartan."

One thing in grade nine that motivated me to look forward to becoming a Sumner Spartan was track. I made the track team, and our practice and track meets were held at Sumner. By the time we arrived there, Sumner's track team would still be practicing. The sophomore members we knew well, but it wasn't long before the juniors and seniors were stars in our eyes, and we could hardly wait to be one of them. It is interesting, almost funny, how things so simple as knowing an old friend is with you, that a girl likes you, and for me, believing I could make a track team, could be such strong motivating forces.

Some of the stars and our mentors at that time are still with us in 2008 A.D. James Blair ran track and later became an outstanding minister of the Gospel, as did one William Thomas. Vernon Coffee, an outstanding Sumner hurdler, became a military officer reaching the rank of colonel. He also became an aide to former President Nixon. Lest we forget, I add the name Alfred House, because he was the first high school boy in Kansas to run a 9.8 second hundred yard dash. In our time that was a feat. I tell you, it was something to see some of our upper classmen. Because of segregation, all Afro-Americans in Kansas City, Kansas, and close surroundings went to Sumner High School. This was the cause of Sumner being a powerhouse of talent, and not just in athletics. Knowing that and having brothers, sisters, and often parents who had gone to Sumner was not just exciting but motivating.

Though my ninth grade was seemingly filled with problems at home, by graduation time the above mentioned motivators somehow removed the early impediments from my mind. Looking back on the year with the understanding and wisdom I now possess, what a different year I would have had - primarily because things at home would have been better. Things would have been better, not because of the absence of problems, but because I would have seen them differently. At the time I was too immature and too inexperienced to know that in life, problems are a constant and how I see them makes the difference.

For example, I now see Aunt Lydia's house as a kind of way station, a place of holding until one can move on to a final destination. Her house was not meant to be our final home. Had I seen that perspective back then, even wrongs could have been perceived differently and my ability to persevere, I suspect, would have been greater.

I recall being sent to an army base in California which held us in tents and Quonset huts. Both of them were uncomfortable for a number of reasons, with overcrowding being one of them. However, because we knew we were merely in a way station, our perseverance and tenacity increased. Oh! How I wish I would have had that view as a teenager.

Last, as a teen, I certainly lacked the spiritual insight that I now have, but what a difference it would have made. Our family conflict back then was viewed as us against uncle, uncle versus us. We lacked spiritual understanding that all of us were not fighting against flesh and blood, but against unseen forces. We could not see that the script our behavior followed was written by those forces. Nor did we know that as long as we were without God, we would continue to follow that script.

The above mentioned mature views were not mine to have on graduation night, but that did not stop me from enjoying the time. The important thing was that I graduated and was heading to Sumner.

FAMILY PHOTOGRAPHS

Eligene as a High School Senior, 1953

Lee Roy at College Graduation. B.S.,Pittsburg State University, 1958

Lee Roy and Eligene, 1987

The Family (l to r):
Eric Wayne Pitts, M.D.; Lee Roy Pitts II;
Lee Roy Pitts, Sr.; Eligene; Jeanette Marie Pitts, M.D.;
Darren Eugene Pitts

Lydia   Lockridge Love (Aunt Lydia) 1893-1968

Charlotte Lockridge Rice (Mama) 1903-1938

Top (L to R): Albert (Bud) Rice, Alberta (Bert) Rice Lewis, Lee Roy Pitts
Bottom (L to R): Madeline (Mat) Carol Pitts Harris; Niece Ella Mae (Sue) Mack; Evelyn (Eve) Delores Pitts Keith

Eric and Karen Joy Pitts and their Children, Erica Joy and Jonathan Irving

Darren & Angela Pitts and their Children, Brandon Xavier and Desirée Alexa

Brandon Xavier Pitts

Jeanette Marie (Gina) Pitts, M.D.

Lee and Theresa Pitts, R.N.

Our Grandson, Lee Roy Pitts III

*Our first
Grandchild, Leah
Sheree, her
Husband, Theo
Coney*

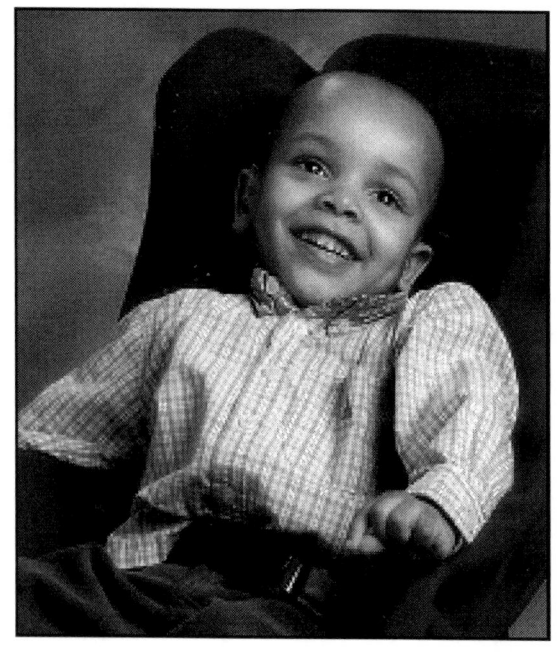

*Our first great-
grandson,
Donovan Josiah
Coney*

Pittsburg State University Relay Team, 1954

Left to Right: Don Davis, Lee Roy Pitts, Ollie Estes, Robert Wooten

CHAPTER VIII

MY GREAT REGRET

As I headed for Sumner High, my optimism was based on my intense desire to achieve and knowing that I had graduated. What I did not know was that I still did not have all the tools in mind to change that script. At least I was at last at Sumner. A number of things were in place at school for me to have a wonderful year. So many classmates I now knew well because some I had been with since grade school and others since the seventh grade. In many cases we already knew who had what talents and gifts. Not to sound arrogant, but in our class there were some very talented students academically and in other areas like fine arts. We had exceptional vocal and instrumental musicians. Time would show the destiny for them that we knew early on. Some became professional. Yet many of them were facing difficult times similar if not identical to mine. It would be some time before we would sense each other's plight.

In my case, my sophomore year started with me and my sister Madeline very much still at odds with our uncle. We had moved to 9 North Second Street and owned the house next door at 11 North Second. Neither house had water or electricity, and soon we discovered both needed roof repairs. That fall money was in short supply, so burning coal was too costly. Therefore, wood was the necessary choice of fuel. I stayed home many days just to look for wood. I remember one time when Aunt Martha Burkehead visited and while there discovered our need. She sent coal to our house. However, my Aunt Lydia would never, as far as I know, initiate a call to voice such a need to her. I noticed very early that it was tacitly taught and understood by my folks, that you were supposed to make it where you were and with what you had, without bothering others with your troubles. Even as a youngster I heard it stated so often. Then and now I believe messages of that kind, whether tacit or otherwise taught, show false pride and are unprofitable. Young people, especially, need a few adults to whom they can voice their troubles. Having adults as mentors and guides helps save young people from many would-be problems.

My sisters Evelyn and Madeline did have some access to our dad's second set of children (we were his third and last set of children). These were older sisters, and they had built a relationship with Mat and Evelyn for a few years by the time I was a mid-teen. More than a few times they went on weekends to stay with one or more of them. Going to stay with them was my sisters' first thought when they were disgusted or at odds with things at home. I never went with them on weekends because, again, I had to cut wood and do other chores.

For me, the start of the school year was the best of times and the worst of times. It was the best because I could envision my possibilities in track and football. I remembered that in the lower grades I was a better sprinter than many if not most my age. So though I had not talked about it, in my thinking it was enough to make other things at school worthwhile.

Some of my worst of times were because the problems and perceived concerns of home were catching up with me, and before Thanksgiving were having a negative impact on my studies. I did not need a mentor to tell me that I needed to be present in classes to be successful. Too often I sat in classes so disgusted about the conflict going on inside me that I seldom concentrated an entire period on what was being taught. Now, with more understanding about life and years of living it, I understand the plight of not only teens having conflict, but adults as well. When you have the ability to do, but for reasons outside of yourself you're unable to accomplish something, then you are provoked to attitudes. Without some help to see that alternatives are possible, you develop an attitude of "what's the use." Then if things persist and insight of hope does not come, often teens begin to act as if they don't care what happens. I know, for I slowly moved that way. After years of working with youth, I have seen this firsthand.

By the end of my sophomore year I came to the conclusion that I had to leave home. I had arrived at the precise frame of mind that my older brother and sister had reached a few years before. I had the will and ability to make it but did not see the way. While walking home from Sumner by myself, I recall thinking about the whole picture of things. I decided that I was getting nowhere in school and catching hell at home. No one would just sit and listen to us teenagers who were crying inside. I might add, talented teens. We were not geniuses, but were definitely gifted enough to make it in school, had our environmental circumstances been better. Later years would prove we were capable children.

On that last day of school that year, I walked east on Oakland Avenue, up the hill to Seventh Street, paused, and looked back at Sumner. I was not satisfied with the year and had the thought that it may be my last. Even with my hurt and disgust, I loved school enough to know that hope for me was in the minds of those teachers in that building. For a while afterwards I was angry, and even in my immaturity blamed a few people, but from the beginning to now, I never blamed my teachers for my circumstances. On the contrary, during those times the most positives I received came from being at school. For a few days, perhaps weeks after the last day of school, I vacillated between disgust, anger, and only the Lord knows what other feelings.

Talking to myself a lot is something I recall doing often. Again and again the "why" question came up regarding home. Then it came up in regard to the school system. I questioned how I could leave Northeast Junior with good grades and one year later have such a down year and absences and nothing in the system would question why. We had no counselors. Recently I visited my old school, and they now have counselors as well as an in-house social worker. As I looked at the diverse student body along with remembering my need at their age, I was overjoyed to see the social worker. Having a number of friends and former students who are social workers, including a nephew and a niece with graduate degrees in social work, I know something of their training and the benefits they give to a community.

For about a month after the last day of school, I tried to see myself going back to school but had not made a final decision. However, something happened that forced the decision.

One day I entered the house to fill the wood box, and a heated altercation was occurring between my sister Madeline and our uncle. She had recently had a baby and was doing quite well. He hit her and she fell to the floor. Spontaneously I hit him. He headed for his bedroom, and I decided that it was best for me to leave. I was hurt for having hit him, hurt for seeing my sister hurt, and I was scared. I was so scared that I think I went through the screen door so fast I took it off the hinges.

The last day of school when I was at Seventh and Oakland, I had the fleeting question of whether I would be able to go to school next year. After the encounter with my uncle, my most regrettable moment had come. Quitting school was and still is my most regrettable decision. I believed my uncle was wrong to have hit my sister as he did, and I was wrong when I hit him. However, acknowledgement of wrong did not negate or remove my deep regret. I would like to have apologized, but when he went to the bedroom I was scared because I knew what he kept under his pillow - his gun. Also I knew my aunt could not handle him when he got angry.

For the rest of that day and a few others I never had much time to worry about where I was going to eat or sleep. Things happened so fast, the only thing I recall doing for a while was walking around in the Bottoms. I do recall going to an ice place called Pasler's to seek work. More than any other thought, I remember saying to myself that I have never lived on "the street" and what am I doing here. Working for Pasler's icing refrigerator cars was too dangerous, I concluded, although I was strong enough to do the job. So I quit after one day of work.

I did get a chance to see how homeless people live, how they must find ways to eat, sleep, and bathe. There were several boys I knew who often robbed the bread man when he left his truck parked while delivering bread and pastries to stores. Thank God I never had that experience or the makeup that would bring it about. My strength was in having experience working. Knowing I could work was calming, but I still felt like a person in exile, that is, no home and on the move to other, unknown places.

Now as I look back, I have looked to see what lessons were learned from all that occurred during the twelve years I lived with my aunt and uncle. Earlier I used the term "way station" to speak of the time of living with them. Certainly that time would be analogous to the way stations I have been in when I was in military service. When I left the country headed to Misawa Airbase in northern Japan, I was sent to Camp Stoneman in Pittsburg, California. It was a way station. When we received orders for Korea, we were sent to a base in southern Japan, which in effect was a holding area.

The rules in a holding area may not be to your liking. Sometimes we didn't like some of the officers or non-coms. Whatever the case, one thing was always in our favor: all of us knew we would only be there an impermanent period of time. With this perspective applied to our time with our aunt and uncle, things could have been so different. At least I can see that my uncle and aunt kept their part of the agreement to keep us. They were not supposed to give up their old fashioned ways of raising children, nor had they raised any children before us. Without help from an outside source, it was lack of knowledge on our part to think things should have been other than the way they were.

One thing I gleaned from the experience was that a person should always look at their circumstance from more than their own perspective. Perhaps in so doing, more insight and wisdom will come. Then one should determine what would be lost if there is change. Is the loss worth it, is an obvious question. In my case I knew leaving home meant a loss of academic knowledge. Immediately after leaving home, there was seldom a time when I was not looking for a way to compensate for that loss. In time I also found that there were some other things I could never recover or replace.

Another thing I learned was that it was important to believe in myself and to be honest, to have integrity in all that I did. Doing that, I found that I could think more clearly, and much of the confusion about what to do became less as I could analyze my situation, my goals, and my limitations. At that time I had no theological position; I was simply attempting to live and make it through each day.

Now as I am nearing the seventy-seven mark in one month, I do have a non-secular or theological and religious belief. When I look back at the opportunities that were mine, doors that opened, people who took a liking to me, I now believe it was the hand of a loving God dispensing grace my way. He saw my honest efforts, my youthful, sometimes crazy mixed-up wrong actions, and through his love, guided me right. I cannot explain all the why questions. Why did he allow me to go wrong, why this and why that, if in the end he was going to guide me right? Now I cannot explain all of that, but I agree fully with St. Paul in Romans 11:33-36 when he says:

Oh, the depth of the riches both of the wisdom and knowledge of God; how unsearchable are his judgments and his ways cannot be tracked out.

For who has known the mind of the Lord? Or who has become his counselor? Or who has first given to him, and it shall be repaid unto him again? Because out of him and through him and unto him are all things. To him be the glory forever. Amen.

When I was a teenager I was blind to other views. I could see that my uncle and aunt were often wrong. They often had views that were not beneficial to youth. What I could not see as a teen was that though wrong in many respects, they had right motives. I believe there was never a time when they did not want what they believed was best for us. I think they believed their views about work were best for children. Like so many of us, they were victims of their generational upbringing. Life in the way station with my aunt and uncle makes sense with the above views. Then with a spiritual eye, pieces came to me.

With that in mind, I can see that it was a good thing to live in the way station in spite of what we went through while there. I was there twelve years, my older brother and sister were there from age twelve to sixteen. None of us came out problem-free, but things could have been worse. None of us ended up on public assistance, none spent time in jail or prison. All of us learned to delay gratification and to work for our livelihood.

Soon after leaving home, I talked with Bill Sappington. He also was ready to leave home. We agreed that our only and best move was to join the military. I do not recall how we decided on what branch of service to join. At least we had settled the issue of whether we would be returning to school the next year. We had not settled the question of how we would get what we would miss by not returning to school.

Leaving home brought relief and hurt. I was hurt when I thought about leaving my two sisters. Later I learned that our oldest sister went to visit the two sisters still at home. Then my sister Mat had recently had a little girl. I had really bonded with this child, and I knew I would miss her greatly.

CHAPTER IX

MILITARY EXPERIENCE

It was a joint decision between Bill and me to join the military. So we joined the United States Air Force. Because of a mix-up in communication between us regarding the time we were to meet at the induction center, Bill was inducted July 11, 1949, and I was sworn in and left on July 12, 1949. Both of us were headed to Lackland Air Force Base in San Antonio, Texas. While traveling to basic training, I had plenty of time to think about all that had occurred in my life. I concluded that I had made a decision, and all that followed would be due to nothing else but my decision - good or bad. I also remember determining that for the rest of my life I would make choices and decisions to benefit me as I had done.

Then I recall settling my anger for my dad. He was not there for us before or after our mother passed, and as I got older, I was angry. I settled that anger, got over it.

En route I also had time to think about our family, my brother and sisters. I knew our problems were not due to an inability to learn. All of us were as smart as many others. I was certain that I was as smart as many of my class. We just lacked the support network that some others had in place.

While I didn't leave home with anything material, I left with something greater still. I left with an attitude that I could survive. My Aunt Lydia constantly said, "God will take care of us." So, as arrogant as it may seem, I always believed in myself and in hard work. I must admit that on the train to basic training, I was not thinking about spiritual help. I was very much an immature young country fellow acting and thinking as such.

Many things came to mind as I rode that train for my first time. I recalled how fortunate I was to have had my Uncle Alf, Alfred Lockridge, with me as long as I had. From the time that mom died until his death in 1947, I do not remember a day without Uncle Alf in my life. This was not so with my dad. I always had male figures in my life in a cousin, Melvin Burkehead, and his dad, Uncle Johnny (John Burkehead). I saw both of them once a week. My cousin Emmett Lockridge, Uncle Alf's son, was available before and after World War II. So although our family structure was without a biological father, I had significant surrogates to allow me normal masculine development.

For basic training I arrived at Lackland Air Force Base in San Antonio, Texas. I was a member of Flight 4297. After being there two weeks, my flight was marching past a mess hall when Bill Sappington ran out and hollered, "Roy!" We were singing as we marched, and he claims he heard and immediately recognized my voice. That evening we were able to get together for a while. We also ran into another Sumner alumnus and graduate of the 1949 class. Clintelle Moore had just graduated from Sumner in May.

The training at Lackland was rough for many, but I enjoyed it. Because of hard work, Bill and I were in some of the best physical shape. Unlike many, I enjoyed the meals. I was used to one-dish meals at home. In basic we had balanced meals. There was meat at every meal, all the milk or juice I wanted, butter, salad, vegetables, bread, and desserts. I remember wanting to sign up for twenty years of this. I enjoyed the classes and the discipline. I enjoyed the marching even when we hurriedly marched across the base to a class, only to have to wait for another flight to leave before we could enter the classroom.

The first day of all this I felt like a rich man when I received clothes. They gave me five pairs of khaki pants and shirts, underclothes, socks, and work and dress shoes. I used to sit on my foot locker and just stare at my clothes hanging neat, ready for inspection. I never had so many clothes in my life. I was in basic training for thirteen weeks, from July 13 to about mid-October, 1949.

Near the end of basic training, I was called to the Orderly Room. There the adjutant explained that they wanted me to remain there as a physical training instructor (PT). He said my other option was to attend Supply Tech School. Fortunately, I had time and got a chance to speak with a Black PT instructor. He explained to me the advantages and disadvantages of going elsewhere and staying there as a PT instructor. I opted for Tech School, and they granted my request. I was selected to go to Supply Tech School at Lowry Field in Denver, Colorado. It was to be a three-month course of study.

At Lowry Field I enjoyed seeing mountains for the first time. The base was not as pretty as Lackland, but it was a beautiful base to be on for longer than my scheduled three months. As soon as we got in class, we became familiar with their main textbook called the Sixty-Seven Dash Four (67-4). In this course we learned how to manage and operate a supply facility from the squadron level to an air base unit. Upon graduation, my Air Force specialty code (AFSC) was supply. Before being discharged, I would attend two other schools of much shorter duration, but Supply remained my main AFSC.

I enjoyed the study, and it did much for my self esteem.

You would need a similar experience to know how I felt on graduation. I had gained the knowledge necessary for going to any air base and have a working understanding of what was supposed to be done in supply at every echelon on the air base. For the first time in my life, I was technically equipped to do a specific job. It was a high point in my life.

After spending time at Camp Stoneman in Pittsburg, California, and the area close by, we boarded a ship and headed north. Since I had left home, I was being educated in many things in many ways. I was surprised that we headed up the coast rather than away from California's west. Soon I learned about great circles and that we were following a great circle to Japan.

I will never forget the feeling I had when we were still aboard the ship and looking out at all the Japanese fishing vessels in the water. As I recall, we disembarked at Yokohoma, Japan. My first night on Japanese soil, I saw masses of people experiencing poverty equal to mine at home and worse.

I had made friends with a Black sergeant named Herbert Ford at Camp Stoneman. He had been in Japan before and was returning after a couple of years. He knew the area and was headed to an area he knew well. Running with Ford allowed me to see more in a short time than I would have alone.

My first assignment was at Misawa Air Base in northern Japan. I was now with the Fifth Air Force. There in the 49th Motor Vehicle Squadron, I worked under a squadron commander named Major Brown, a West Point graduate. I was under a unit leader named Walter H. Dorrer. Dorrer was a master sergeant as permanent rank, but with temporary rank of captain in World War II. Dorrer already had more time in service than both our squadron commander and our group commander, who was a Bird Colonel and a non-flying officer.

When I arrived at the supply unit in Misawa, there was master sergeant Dorrer, one tech sergeant, and one staff sergeant. Arriving with me was another airman who would become a good friend. He was John G. Huefel of Dade City, Florida. The Tech Sergeant Newhouse was soon to be leaving for the States. Staff sergeant Duggan would be with us for a while. He would become a good friend also, a person to whom I could speak unofficially about what concerned me.

Sergeant Dorrer took John and me, recent graduates of Supply Tech School, and began to teach us all the tricks of the trade, particularly what was not in the tech manuals and regulations. He told us that for every regulation that told us what and how to do something, there were ways to get around all of them. Dorrer knew loopholes that few others had thought about. Inasmuch as my Uncle Alfred was a survivor and possessor of similar skills, I took to Dorrer like a fly on flypaper. There were a number of times when he would share a scenario and ask the two of us what we would do or what was possible. He began to like my answers, and soon could see that I had the finesse to avoid most obstacles and regulations in order to accomplish what he wanted. He would have a certain little grin which I knew meant he was pleased. He liked my mental adroitness and teachableness.

Needless to say, I made rank very fast under this man who recommended me. Whatever the test or questions, he would have his people ready. At nineteen I was one of the youngest buck sergeants in our outfit. At that time the old guys were still saying buck sergeant for three stripes. In Air Force lingo, the correct language is airman first class and represented as A/1C.

In addition to having learned how to apply my Tech School knowledge from the Sergeant, I also learned something far more important to me for my future plans. I had learned how military politics would sometimes work. I had seen and experienced favoritism as stated. By extension of similar thinking, I could envision working under some leader who was not so inclined to fairness. For me at the time it would have been an awful experience, not to mention the financial loss. So whereas I once thought about staying in the service, at least I then saw the advantages and now the disadvantages as well.

Master Sergeant Dorrer was the one who made me aware of the military general educational development test (GED). He gave me time off to study for it. Daily I went to the Information and Education Building (I & E) to study, and later it was there I took the battery of tests. There were a number of us who took the exams. When the results came in, we reported to the I&E building, and the I&E officer gave us copies of our results. I was glad to learn that I had passed all five sections of the exams and scored above the national average on all phases. He went over the test and explained what percentiles meant. He also made us aware of the United States Armed Forces Institute (USAFI) courses available on the base and through correspondence. Later, while speaking with him one-on-one, I learned of a school in Chicago, fully accredited by the North Central Association of Schools and Colleges, where one could take high school courses by correspondence. I also learned that some state universities offered high school courses. At the time I had no knowledge of what accredited schools meant.

I was still determined to receive what I had missed by dropping out of school; therefore I enrolled in a school in Chicago called the American School. My first courses were

American History, Psychology, Algebra, and Parliamentary Procedures. When the Korean War started on June 25, 1950, further studies were interrupted when we prepared for mobilization and move to Korea. Although I had passed the GED, what I wanted was coursework similar to what I had missed. At the time I did not know that the GED would be applicable in the civilian sector upon discharge.

After having had both coursework for the GED and classroom setting, I do not believe they are the same. I believe the GED is very valuable and should be available to those who need it. However, I believe the GED is for emergencies. If the opportunity to stay in school is there, one should avail oneself of that opportunity. It is a mistake to drop out simply because the GED is available. Often in history we find the young tripped up by new fads when the new thing is used in the wrong way.

Master Sergeant Dorrer helped those under him to improve. I was grateful for his guidance and fairness to me. The record would probably show that John Huefel and I, in addition to being the last to come into the squadron, were also probably the youngest. I noticed that Sergeant Dorrer and our First Sergeant, Master Sergeant Funk, seemed to take us under their observation and make sure we were developing in a way that would allow us to be promoted without trouble. They both had enough hash marks on their arms to indicate that they were career soldiers. Both were determined to see to it that we could be also if we so desired.

Dorrer had been a flying officer in World War II. When the Korean War started, our squadron commander, Major Brown, himself a flying officer, suggested that Dorrer apply for reinstatement to his temporary Captain rank and flying status. Within a short time, we were saluting our new Captain.

A number of our squadron were scheduled to ship out for Korea with Major Brown and Captain Dorrer. However, as soon as Captain Dorrer was checked out on our F-80 saber jets, he left with Major Brown and other flying officers for Korea. The rest of us left within a month or so with supplies and continued to take supplies between Japan and Korea. It was a new experience, learning to mobilize for war, but a fascinating one.

To travel throughout the Far East was an education in itself. Learning the cultures so different than ours at home, yet finding people's basic needs the same as our own, was really a confirmation of my upbringing in the Bottoms. I am glad that I took the time to travel the length and breadth of Japan. I talked with young and old. Old men told me about their views about World War II before and after the war. Then I spoke with men about how they felt seeing their women with soldiers in illicit relationships. As I look back, even I am surprised when I think of how gutsy I was to venture into some places just to see what was what. I grew up poor, but in the Far East I saw poverty like never before. With my early childhood experience I had become sensitive to human needs by the time I left home. Living abroad deepened that sensitivity.

After my tour of duty in the Far East, I was sent to Aberdeen Proving Grounds, an army base, and prepared to be discharged. Most of us had our tours extended for a few months up to a year because of the need by the service. Since with a few exceptions, service had been good for me, reenlisting would be an option. Military discipline and the feeling of doing something productive made me feel good and raised my self esteem. I liked the growth I had made, but still, the decision to leave or stay in service would not be made lightly. I had enough experience by then to look objectively at the pros and cons of military service. As I said, I had been closely involved with both commissioned and noncommissioned officers. I had experienced good ones and some who, by most standards, were not fit for the title they wore. Mainly I needed to consider my goals, needs, and reasons for wanting to leave the service. At that time I still thought my greatest need was academic education, whether I remained in the service or left.

Bill and I entered service at a time when we both wanted to be in school. One part of our life was closed out, but all was not lost. Entering service, we found another world of opportunity. The military offered a different kind of education. The travel itself was an exposure worth much to us.

I missed out on many things shortly after leaving school. It was not long before I acknowledged that some things missed I could never retrieve or relive. For example, I missed the social interactions with classmates at Sumner High School. Then I missed the contribution I could have made to the athletic achievement of my class, especially in track and field. Equally missed was the opportunity to be involved in extracurricular activities such as dramatic plays for student development. I recall seeing a football game and a play while on furlough, and I had to leave the football game early - such was the emotion and hurt from thinking I could have been playing. Then knowing the kind of teachers we had had caused me to know what I missed in that sense.

I must add that years later the opportunity would be mine to experience the philosophy and minds of a few of those teachers I had missed. When I became a teacher in the Kansas City, Kansas, school system, a few of those teachers were still active. I got a chance to talk with a number of them at district meetings.

On my last furlough I spent Christmas with the young lady who had been so special to me in junior and senior high school. She was attending Kansas City University and working at the home of the chancellor. We had such a wonderful time together, but little did we know that the war would keep me away more than a year, too long, and our lives took different directions.

The furlough before my last I had seen another young lady of interest and was introduced to her by Sandra Doniphan, a classmate of mine. I only had the chance to speak with her briefly. It escapes me how I got her address, but I did. When I returned to base overseas I wrote her. I had only briefly spoken to her and I really did not expect a response, but I was upset when I did not receive one. My expectations were not fulfilled, and I felt the loss because I really liked what I saw in this girl. When I saw her again, she gave me some story as to why she didn't write me. Since I believed my experience had taught me that absence makes the heart grow fonder for those who are nearby, I really didn't believe her story.

So after three years, three months, nineteen days, six hours, and about fifteen minutes of devoted service to my country in the uniform of the United States Air Force, I left the service. With an honorable discharge, I left with thanks because I was unable to do in civilian life what I had done in part in the military. Before service I had the will to attend school but did not have the way. Now on leaving military service, I still had the will, and now I also had the monetary way to go to school. I left service with one question on my mind: How can I get my education? I had a made-up mind not to waste my GI bill entitlement.

CHAPTER X

MY BEST EVER DECISION

On my arrival in Kansas City, I began to look for careers in which I could invest my GI Bill eligibility. I knew I also needed a job immediately. Having been overseas for a number of years, things looked so different, but I soon began to reconnect with the area and old friends. I did not reconnect with the old girlfriend.

My aunt Rebecca Vincson told me she had some influence that could get me on the Highway Patrol. I also found that the training received in service would not make me eligible for jobs because segregation was still rampant and affecting employment for minorities. So I started concentrating on going to school.

Since grade school I was interested in art, and according to the arts supervisor, Miss Cardwell, I showed an aptitude for art. She had taken a picture I had done and placed it on exhibit in the public library. Also in my family I was certain artistic talents showed. My brother Albert could draw portraits that looked like photographs when he got through touching the eyes. My sister Mat could draw very well. Mat and my sister Alberta drew designs on cloth before embroidering pillowcases. Our mother was a professional seamstress who could take a picture of a dress and measurements of a person and cut her pattern.

With all of that in mind and my liking art, I decided to make application to the Kansas City Art Institute. I was accepted and spent only one semester. I had not been in an art class or drawn for five years. To work and practice, I concluded, there would not be enough time to make up what I had missed in years past. Then I noticed different levels and types of students there. There were some who seemingly were only there because there was little else for them to do. Certainly there were a few really good students that, barring something unusual, were going somewhere in the field of art. A Hispanic friend from the Bottoms was in this latter category, for he did ascend the heights. He became well known as "Tavi." One of my high school classmates, Sandra Doniphan, was also exceptional and at the Institute when I attended.

Fortunately, near the end of that semester I met with a VA counselor/advisor. He shared with me the benefits of attending a college or university where I could get two years of broad general education before specialization in some area. That sounded good to me. On learning that I had been involved with Cartography in the military, he also told me about jobs with the Federal government. There I found the Army Map Service, a branch of the Corps of Engineers. I applied there, took the test, and took the job when it was offered a short time later. I stayed there and was promoted on time. My supervisor, Mr. Acosta, said my work was very good and soon gave me more complex tasks.

The Corps of Engineers was an excellent place to work, and had I already had college, I would have remained. As it was, I remained there until I was fairly certain of the college to which I would seek entrance. Before and during my work at the Corps, I was still trying to have more contact with Eligene Clay, who I had met on furlough. I had written her, but she had not responded. However, the path to my really getting to know her happened through the channel of the church people. At the time I could never have visualized the many good unplanned things that caused me to get to know her. While I did my part in pursuing her, I am glad that other things were favorable to me.

On my last furlough, something unplanned happened that significantly affected me and my future. It occurred one evening when an older lady with whom I was staying asked me if I would go to church with her before I returned to service. I was on a 30-day furlough and did not plan on spending any of it in church. At that time I was not much of a churchgoer. On the base I went to chapel service now and then. At my age I thought I didn't need church. Nevertheless, I told this sweet lady, Sister Lena Glover, that I would. However, I had not planned on going. I was aware of her work hours. She got home about 5 o'clock or later sometimes. I knew I would be gone by then and I could dodge her for 30 days.

As fate would have it, one Wednesday she was home early and caught me heading out the door. With her soft angelic voice, she said, "Roy, would you like to go with me tonight, we have a revival and a good speaker." So I said to myself, I may as well go and get this old lady off my back."

To her I said, "Yes, ma'am," so I took my then hypocritical, lying self to church. There was singing going on, songs I had not heard since I was a child, at Freeman Avenue Church of God. From where I sat in the back, I could only see the pastor, a large man, whom I would later know and love very much, sitting on the rostrum.

When they introduced the speaker, I still could not see her because she was sitting in the chair immediately behind the tall pulpit. To my surprise, the one introducing her said,

"Our own Sister Alberta Lewis," my oldest sister. She couldn't see me and I couldn't see her. Because I was sitting behind someone, she still couldn't see me well and not expecting me also kept her from seeing me. When she spoke, I found her to be still articulate, forceful in her delivery, still persuasive in her logic. Her message was believable and got through to me.

However, during the course of her sermon and before her conclusion, I took issue with some things that she said and how she said them. I received the statements personally and got angry because I thought my business was being put before everyone. Before she finished, even with my anger I had time to think about the good that had happened to me overseas and some of what could have happened. I knew that a personal friend and classmate, William Reynolds, had been killed and his body had been shipped back to Kansas City, Kansas. I had known him since seventh grade, and he was a really nice and good friend. I was personally hurt to learn about that before I left for home. So things were right for me to hear the conclusion and closing of the sermon.

During those years, after each sermon the practice at Third Street Church of God was to have an altar call. It was an opportunity for people who wished to make a public statement or have someone pray with them regarding some concern. It was decision-making time. For some time I had been pondering a number of concerns: to stay in service or not, how to get to school, and things in general about returning to civilian life soon. At the moment of the sermon closing, those thoughts merged with knowing that God had been good to me. While I was still standing, concealed from view of the speaker, I was touched on the arm by a lady. Sister Ethel White touched me and asked if I would like to go forward for prayer.

Before the touch, it was what my sister said in closing that caused me to rehear the whole sermon's intent. It was the intent of the sermon put forward that stimulated an honest examination of where I was and where I wanted my life to go. I decided to try my sister's way of living and accept the Christ of her sermon. I went forward, though my mind was made up before I stepped out. I did not know the how or what was coming next, but I knew I was serious about my decision.

My sister was surprised to see me but overjoyed about my decision. In one month I will be seventy-seven years of age. In that number of years I have made many decisions, but I know the decision I made that night was my best ever decision. That is true because all that I am and all that I hope to be is based on the Christ in that decision. It is interesting that the person through whom the Lord worked to open my mind/eyes was my big sis. I loved her so.

At the time that I made my decision to follow the teachings of Christ, I was not thinking about pleasing anyone other than myself. However, that decision, perhaps more than any other thing, put me in a favorable position to date Eligene because of the church teaching and belief that marriages were better when both persons were of the same faith tradition. I was attracted to her for several reasons. Also I was very cautious because if she just didn't like me, I was not going to continue and be hurt or embarrassed. Later I found her reasons for not writing me to be valid from her perspective. I was glad the door had opened for a relationship to start to get to know each other.

I learned that she was being pulled in other ways. So our relationship was slowed. Part of that was due to her work hours. She worked at the University of Kansas Medical Center emergency room from 3:00 p.m. to 11:00 p.m. This did not leave much room for socializing, since she was still a senior at Sumner High School. Because of problems with her dad, she had left home and was on her own.

My big opportunity to get with her came one Wednesday evening. It was her day off, and she attended midweek church service. When she came out of service, I was about to leave, but when I saw her I asked if she would like to go for a walk or get a cone. She said yes. Next came what I have since called "our walk that bonded us." We left Third and Richmond, went west on Richmond to Fifth Street. South on Fifth Street to Washington Boulevard, then west to Twelfth to Grant's BBQ. During our walk we talked about many things and discovered some of our likes and dislikes. We ate something at Grant's, but I do not remember what. I remember enjoying the moment, her smile and disposition, and it all made it a wonderful evening for me. It had been some time since I had dated a girl with class; then Grant's was always a nice place to take a classy lady.

I was always direct in my inquiry. I asked her whether she was involved with somebody else. She said she was not. After that night we began to spend as much time together as possible. We shopped together, sometimes went to church together. We drove around in a pickup truck often - just riding. We had come a long way since the first time I saw her ironing at Sister Glover's house. At that time I was on furlough and living upstairs. Eligene was in her senior year, first semester.

Before our relationship had gotten very far, I recall some older ladies in the church decided to match make. Separately we were invited to a dinner where we thought other young people would be present. After we got there we knew what was happening. They were trying to be nice and doing what they thought best for their sweet young teen lady of the church. They had known Eligene since her early teens. They had known my family for years and so were sure they knew me. We were still grateful to them, but we really didn't cement our relationship until sometime later.

Both of us had dated before that. There was quite a lot of contrast in our experiences. At least this was true as expressed. I had dated several girls and was in a serious relationship with one, and with that one believed I was in love. Eligene, on the other hand, never believed she was ever in love with any of the young men with whom she had either had a date or a close relationship. Certainly, I was supposed to believe her because she was a young, pretty "walk on water" Christian. She knew I didn't, and we would laugh about it. I knew she had the kind of outgoing personality and most people took to her, both men and women.

It was at Kansas University Medical Center when I really found out what kind of person she was. She worked from 3:00 to 11:00 p.m. in the emergency room. One night we had just boarded a public transit bus heading home when at least two ambulances passed the bus. We had not traveled a complete block when she jumped up and hurriedly went to the front door to get off. I said, "You just got off work and we just paid the fare." In my mind I was also thinking, "which I can't get back." We got off and all she kept saying while walking fast was, "They are shorthanded tonight and they need me." As I sat in the emergency room waiting for over an hour, I had time to think about what had just happened and what it meant to me. I became aware through firsthand knowledge that this girl really tried to live according to high ethical principles. More important, I was aware that I liked what I saw in her.

As I look back, that was a crazy unstable period in our lives. She had the concern about her mother heavy on her mind. Also she was living away from home on her own and working. Meanwhile I was planning on going to school and wanted her to go with me. Sometimes our lack of total communication because of so much going on caused us to be apart, then together, then apart. Sometimes I wouldn't remember what had caused the breakup. I just remember always wanting things to clear up between us because I was sure I had been bitten by the "in love" bug. Deeper still, all the problems going on were not between us but rather what was pulling on both of us. I think we knew neither of us wanted anyone else but needed to let the clouds clear on things in general.

CHAPTER XI

MY UNDERGRADUATE
COLLEGE DAYS

While Gene was working to help resolve some of her family concerns, I was working to bring closure to my plans for school. My plans originally had her going to school with me but now was not to be the time.

I had written letters to several universities and was waiting for a response. Then I recalled Miss Caldwell (later Swisher) one of my former teachers at Northeast Junior, had attended Kansas State Teachers College at Pittsburg, Kansas. So I decided and left for Pittsburg, arriving one evening. I had an army duffel bag containing some military clothes and a couple of civvies. Someone told me where the Caldwells lived, and I headed in that direction.

When I arrived at the house, I was greeted by a sister of Miss Caldwell named Dolly. I told her I was a former student of her sister and wanted to know where I could get a room for the night. She said it was late and I probably couldn't at that hour. Afro-Americans could not stay in hotels. She offered me a sofa bed located in an unattached garage in the rear of the house. The garage had no door. I certainly could understand her not letting me enter her home because she didn't know me, in spite of my telling her I knew her sister Miss Caldwell. I appreciated her help.

The next morning she told me how to get to the college and wished the best for me. I told her thanks for her help and what a pleasure it was to meet Miss Caldwell's sister. She was as beautiful as I remembered Miss Caldwell to be. Before graduation I would meet their dad and all the family when Miss Caldwell returned during a summer vacation back home.

I went to a service station, washed up, and headed to the college. When I arrived I saw students heading to one of the buildings. After speaking with several of them, I learned they were first-time students. They knew where we were to go. School was to begin later in the fall, but exams were being given for students with special situations. I was eventually admitted on the basis of that exam. Thinking the GED test I passed in the military was just for military, I never mentioned it nor did I have a copy. Later I learned they would have admitted me on the basis of that exam. I did send for and received a copy of my GED results from my military files.

After inquiring about my background, the professor giving the exam took me to the athletic building. I was introduced to the track coach, Mr. Prentice Gudgen. He wanted to know what I had done in sports and when. Then I walked around and started getting acquainted with the campus. It was too late to get a room in the dormitory because these rooms were pre-assigned. Then for minorities there was only one room on each floor for us. I was sent to an office where I was given an address of a couple that took in boys. It was located at 312 West Forest, some distance from the college. A very nice Black couple lived in and managed the house. After I met with them, they did rent me the room. I could sleep there with bath privileges and no cooking.

Needless to say, I was just glad to have a room in which to sleep.

In a day or so I enrolled, received my schedule of classes, got my books, and went to locate the rooms where my classes would be held. I was not expecting to see anyone that I knew, but soon ran into several former Sumner High School students. One was a classmate of mine. She remembered me and was very friendly. I had forgotten that a number who graduated in May 1951 were still in college in 1954. Catherine Cade was one of several I would soon see, and all of my classmates were seniors. There were a still larger number of other students from Sumner. Many of them were from the 1953 class, the class of my wife-to-be, but I didn't know them. In all cases the students were friendly and helpful to me and others just starting college.

Several asked me what was going to be my major and proceeded to tell me what professors to avoid. One professor's name came up a number of times as one to avoid. I was told directly that Dr. Theodore Sperry in the Biology department was to be avoided at all costs. Word had spread among Black students that he was prejudiced and among students in general that he was just tough and hard to satisfy. Later I had to take Dr. Sperry because he was the only teacher of a subject I needed. Since Pittsburg was a small college, that happened more often than in large colleges and universities.

After being in Dr. Sperry's class listening to his lectures and observing his behavior toward students, I formed my own views of Dr. Sperry. Later when I ran into some who had told me to avoid him and they discovered I was enrolled in his class, they immediately said, "Didn't you hear about Dr. Sperry ?" I shared my view of the man based on personal experience. I told them they should stop going around telling folks that Dr. Sperry was prejudiced and didn't like

Black students. I told them my observation caused me to conclude that Dr. Sperry didn't like anybody. He treated all students the same. He would just as soon tell a white student boy or girl where to go or some such snappy retort to a decent intelligent question. I do not know many who enjoyed being in his class. As one fellow said, on hearing that Dr. Sperry had died, "I don't think too many tears are going to be dropped for Dr. Sperry." In short, Dr. Sperry was a very knowledgeable teacher, sharper than many, but his pedagogical skills and approaches in handling and relating to people were, in my opinion, seriously flawed beyond those of many college teachers I have had during undergraduate and graduate times.

Such neglectful teaching often continues for years, with students complaining while administrators ignore it or feel powerless to remove such people. So year after year students go to college with ready minds, only to be exposed to such "put down" teaching. Students expect knowledgeable teachers but also teachers with wisdom. Their only recourse is to talk about it to fellow students if it is a small school. At a larger institutions one can usually take a course from another professor.

I am glad to see more Christian colleges and universities developing and offering students a sound education from teachers who realize the needs of the students sitting before them.

Fortunately, with the military behind me, I had the necessary background and tenacity to sit in difficult teachers' classes and get what I needed to complete my degree. However, tenacity notwithstanding, many of us had our fill of a few teachers who did not want us there and had their way of letting us know it. I know of more than a few who sat in classes where instructors believed Blacks were not capable of making As and Bs, so they suffered under that philosophical ignorance. Such interactions often hurt us, as it limited us to taking the bare essentials from some teachers. In the case of Dr. Sperry, by the time I got him in grad school, it was still more of the same type of teaching.

It is interesting that in that same department was a professor whose name would exude a good teacher image in the minds of those who had his classes. He was Dr. Horace H. Hayes, a zoologist. He was as balanced a teacher as any at our college. He was one of those who went the extra mile to help all students. He was demanding in his class requirements, but also encouraging to those whose backgrounds may have been weak in the sciences. He was always approachable and did not act one way in his office and different outside on campus. I know of no student that did not speak highly of him.

Some years ago I returned to campus, and he was getting ready to retire. He was giving away items in his office library. I have his personal copy of Comparative Anatomy of Vertebrates from when he was a student in college. In recent years he was brought to Kansas City to be hospitalized. I went to see him, thinking since it was some time since he had seen me, that he would not remember me. I slowly approached his bedside. As I looked down on him, he turned his head my way, looked at me, and with his characteristic Alfred Hitchcock voice, said "Lee, Roy, Pitts." He smiled and I had a big grin also.

When I left his room I left my name and telephone number at the nurses' station. I told them if he needed anything nonmedical that he could have and wanted, please call me. A nurse told me that he must be a wonderful man, because there had been several others who came and voiced the same sentiment. I told her he helped a lot of students in many ways. That fine man was nothing short of a blessing for many of us because one had to have at least General Biology for a degree. He was a bright star in the Biology department.

Most departments had at least one or two professors who worked hard to bring minorities like Afro-Americans, foreign students, and any other disadvantaged student, up to par in their class. As I stated, they did not change their requirements, but like Dr. Hayes, talked with you to determine your need and guided you.

There was one department at Pittsburg that seemed to be exemplary and had more professors who showed themselves to be concerned and good teachers. Our Social Science department was one of the best. I was not a social science major or minor, but I did have classes from three professors in that department. These professors lived up to their name - they were indeed social. They were tough and very tough, pouring the work on. Though the work was very challenging to me, my interest level caused me to enjoy all the courses I took. Had I gotten involved with this department my first year, I can see myself having selected that as a major. Since it was completely new to me and my reading speed was not up until my second year, it is good that I didn't go into that area.

In the Social Science department was Dr. Elizabeth Cochran. Anyone who took a course from her and made an A or B probably could do the same in any college or university in the world. I wrote my first formal paper under her supervision. When I think of all the teachers I have had in undergrad and graduate school, this lady would be at the top in two ways. First, she was a no-foolishness, no-jive teacher. Equally, she was tops in knowing her subject - history. It was often said if Paul Revere's horse would have had a name, Dr. Elizabeth Cochran would have known what it was. She was so full of history she made me interested in reading the tough reading assignments. Believe me, you could not fool her or fake that you did all the assigned reading. If you didn't do the reading or turn in your reports of reading, it would show up on your exams. If you slacked off, your exams would look like they had blood dripping from them. After attending five colleges and universities, Dr. Cochran is still the toughest teacher I have had. Still, like others in her department she was helpful and fair. I do not think she had an ounce of prejudice in her.

Another professor that we loved for his support and understanding of Afro American students was Dr. Dudley T. Cornish. We could rely on him to sponsor activities when a faculty member was needed. He wrote a book entitled The Negro Soldier in the Civil War.

Then there was "The Dr. Robert Noble" from whom I took a course titled "Marriage and Family." I had many conversations with Dr. Noble, and a conversation with him was time well spent. Many were the times the topic of the lecture was continued after class, where I had opportunity to bring up other related issues. He would evoke deeper conversation.

As I said, had I taken social science classes the first year and had my reading been up, I would have enjoyed social science. In all the courses I took in that department, more than just the textbook was required . Many reference books were used. By my sophomore and junior year, my reading speed was up, but by then I had already started work in another major field. I had three years of GI Bill entitlement, so I had to get finished. All of that good stuff in social sciences I would have to read later. Since graduating I have done just that, read widely in the social and psychology area. I have friends who teach in those fields who keep me informed as to what is being read.

The worst enemy I had as a minority was not teachers who gave tough exams. Rather, it was those teachers who did not want us on campus, let alone in their class. As stated, a few were bold enough to let us know in ways quite evident how they felt. However, there was always good lurking nearby.

Countering those few who worked to be impediments in our development were those whose view of humankind and teaching philosophy helped us to press on to our degrees. It was those teachers and deans who advised and gave guidance to us. Some were even there with funds. Just from my own memory experience, I list a few I do not want to forget: Dr. Ralph Wright, Dean of Students; Dr. Horace Hays - Biology; Dr. Morgan and Dr. Morgan, father and son - professors in Engineering and Industrial Technology; Dr. Noble; Dr. Cochran; Dr. Cornish - Social Science; Dr. Wells - Chair, Biology; Dr. J. Carl Bass - Limnology; Dr. J. D. Haggard - Mathematics; Dr. Smith - Mathematics; Jack Overman - Student Union Manager.

Those professors became significant other persons in my life. They were tough, as I stated, but to their credit and our benefit, at least they did not try to flunk us out before we got started, unlike a few we can name. Mr. Jack Overman, manager of the student union, was always helpful. A few times my GI check was late, and when I went to him, he allowed me to eat until the check came. In 2008 I returned to college for a fifty year out of college celebration, and it was good to see Mr. Overman, now 90 years of age and as active as ever. We were surprised to hear him call a few names as we shook hands and embraced.

At college I soon learned of programs and activities to add to student development. Such activities also served to give us a change of pace from the rigors of academic study. There were a few that interested me. During my first semester I decided to become part of the YMCA on campus. It served as a kind of church away from home. All of the boys who attended the meetings were Christians and behaved as such. Therefore I was comfortable and enjoyed attending. It gave me new friends on campus. One of my old friends from Sumner, Lezell Smith, also attended Y meetings. It really was an uplift.

I remember well one winter day we had a cookout of just baked beans and hot dogs. We sang fun songs. It was like Boy Scout camps my boys would later experience. One thing I thought unusual for a secular college was meeting my first math teacher there - Dr. J. D. Haggard.

My sophomore year I got involved in student government as a member of the Human Relations Council. My cousin Janet Gains Hopkins served on that council also. That year I also became part of a choir formed in years past by Afro-American students. The choir was called the Choraleers and existed for fun, fellowship, and survival. On Sundays we had no place to eat since the college offered no service, and places in town serving real meals did not serve Afro-Americans. So on Sundays we traveled to nearby small towns and sang in Black churches. Many there were older Blacks who knew experientially our situation. Therefore after service in songs they had wonderful balanced meals for us. Often we were able to take food back to the dorm for an evening snack. We were recipients of their understanding and love. These folks were future oriented in that they wanted things better for us then, but in the future as well. Looking back now as a senior with more understanding, I know without doubt that meeting these good old people was definitely one of many unexpected encounters with God's Grace.

We primarily sang Negro spirituals, and, without bragging, we were good. One of my grade school friends, Clarence Cole, was our director. The conception of the Choraleers happened a few years before I arrived at Pittsburg. One of the founders was Mr. John Drew, a former Sumner High School graduate and one of Kansas City, Kansas's great baritones.

My most memorable and most cherished extracurricular activity was track and field. I met and made friends with some fellows who became lifelong friends. We have scattered to many parts of the world, but when we returned for a recent reunion, we greeted each other with warm smiles and hugs. We shared what we had been doing these many years. Some of our teammates are: Don Davis, Robert Wooten, Ollie Estes, Eddie West, Rose Evans, Henry Scott, Ralph Handley, Melvin Coates, David Suenram, Lee Crawford, and a number of others. These guys were good athletes, and it was a joy to be a teammate of theirs.

In Japan and before the Korean War I had the opportunity to meet many good runners from all around the world. Then when I returned to the States and the East Coast, I met some Olympians. I was stationed at Aberdeen Proving Grounds Army Base and had time to travel in the area. One of the best and finest athletes I have met was Andrew Young of Atlanta. He became a minister, ambassador to the United Nations, and one of the best 200 meter runners of the time.

However, with all that I've seen, my favorite runner is my running mate and friend, Robert Wooten. Sometimes we called him Bob, sometimes Bobbie. But he is Mr. Robert Wooten. To see him run a 200 or a quarter mile was a sight to see. Bob and I were known to be of the even tempered types. I think Bob's frustration tolerance is higher than mine. On our half-mile relay I usually ran the third leg, so I was handing off to Bob. That meant I could see his entire race.

Another teammate I will never forget is David Suenram. David was the most serious man on our team as well as the hardest worker. I loved his competitive spirit. Whatever David was involved in, he studied for improvement. He went on to become head coach of track of Pittsburg, and I think one of the best. I admire David.

Eddie West was an exceptional all-around athlete. He participated in football and track. In addition to being a good athlete, nature endowed him with "smarts," good looks, and a wonderful personality to go with the former. Ed was also even tempered but highly competitive.

Melvin Coates was the kind of guy anyone would want on their team. I thought Mel was one of the most gifted athletes I have known. He was extremely competitive and a matter-of-fact guy. Always you could depend on him to do what was needed. He was a fine hurdler and could sprint with the best of us. If you blinked your eyes wrong or had a lapse of thought for a moment in a 200 meter, Melvin would beat you. It was a pleasure to run with Mel and now still know him as my fine friend. He too was an intelligent guy. Like David, Melvin had no prejudice; he treated folks with fairness. He would tell you if he messed up, but also would tell you if you messed up and didn't pull your load. I appreciated and liked Melvin Coates, who became a principal in Wichita, Kansas.

These fellows that I've mentioned would have made any track team in the United States, as would I. I really think several of our guys could have been pushed at a larger school to try out for the Decathlon. I think Eddie West, Melvin Coates, and David Suenram would have been good candidates.

Where do I fit in with these guys? Well, most of them saw me as one of the best sprinters. I was the second fastest, with Bob Wooten being our fastest. Mel, with a big smile, would say he could beat us both, even though the clock talked a different story. That's the kind of competitive spirit that made us have a good team.

My contribution was in running the open 100 hundred and 200 meters. Often I ran the 200 in the sprint medley. Always I ran on the 4 x 100 and the 4 x 200. Sometimes I ran on the 4 x 400. I admit I think Bob and I would rather run the 200 meter than eat.

Second behind the 200 meter is my love for the relays. In 1957 we walked off with first place in the 4 x 100 and the 4 x 200 relays at the Texas Relays in Austin, Texas. Then at Drake Relays the same year, we won the 4 x 200 meter relay. To stand on the victory stand with the American flag and others flying, with thousands in the stands watching, was a high point in my college days.

One good thing about our team was I do not remember any racial friction on our team. Another thing that is a high point to me is to know that all of us, to the best of my knowledge, received our degrees on time. We were not "dumb jocks." Nor did we get degrees in "basket weaving," but in areas where we could become employed. As I was speaking with Bob Wooten recently, he voiced the sentiments of many of us. He said he went to college because for him college was a way out of poverty. My sentiments exactly.

During my freshman year I was running in a track meet at Emporia State University. While waiting for a race, I heard someone in the stands say, "Lee Roy." It was a high school classmate, Hargest Shumate, now Dr. Shumate, retired elementary principal. It was so good to see him. He also had been in military service and returned to college. In high school he played basketball, football, and ran track. There at Emporia State he was on the basketball team. He experienced similar prejudices there, as we did, and also when they traveled. He could not stay with the team in hotels. I had seen few girls from my high school class and fewer boys, so seeing him was a real plus. Both of us ended up in the education field and have since retired after forty and fifty years of service. Hargest is one of the finest gentleman I know. As fate would have it, both of us belong to the same college fraternity.

Participating in track in the military and college provided invaluable opportunities to travel and meet people I would never have known . For example, I first saw Wilt Chamberlain at Kansas University Relays. I was leaning against a wall waiting for the call for the 4 x 200 relay when I saw this waistline pass near my eye level. I took a double take and asked who was that. That was the first ever I heard his name. We met him personally later at the Drake Relays, since both teams were housed in the same hotel.

During the times in which we were in college, things were usually no different on campus than in the larger society. We experienced societal prejudices as we traveled to track meets. When we went to East Texas for a meet, the Afro-Americans of our team could not run or participate in any events. We sat in the spectator section while our teammates did well but lost the meet.

Then we traveled to the Texas Relays in Austin, Texas. There, Afro-Americans could not stay in motels or hotels. Our large bus went down some dirt road off the main street for some fifteen minutes. It stopped in front of a house and Prentice Gudgen said, "You boys will stay here." The homeowner was a nice lady named Mrs. Miller. I noticed that the outside of the house, while not extremely bad, could have used some upkeep, contrary to the inside. Inside her home was not only well kept, but there was beautiful and modern furniture.

When all the guys went into town, I remained to write Gene. Curiosity got the best of me, so I asked Mrs. Miller why the difference between the outside and inside. She told me that it was her way of surviving. She said if whites thought you were not doing well they would often help by giving you things. That if her home look too good, she learned that she fared less well. She was an older woman whose background equipped her to be observant, and so she developed her own perception of how to cope.

When we returned to our campus, I spoke with the coach about our split from the white teammates. He told me that there was little he thought he could do. I disagreed and told him so vehemently. It was true that there was little need to worry about what we experienced down there one time per year, when things were not right every day on our own campus and in the city of Pittsburg. We returned home to dormitories where, as already stated, there were prescribed rooms in each dorm on each floor for Black students. I stayed in Tanner Hall, 218, and we all got to know which one room on each floor and in each dorm was ours, so to speak.

Such times existed on campus and in the larger society in too many places. The same policies were in force at other state colleges in Kansas. My classmate, Hargest Shumate, a member of the basketball team at Emporia State, said they went to Kansas City, Missouri, to play in the Municipal

Auditorium and stay in the hotel Muehlbach. The hotel is about one block or less away from the auditorium. That mattered not to Hargest, because he had fare to ride public transit cross-town so he could stay at home and not with the team.

We had to learn how to cope with the wrongs we could not change in order to accomplish our goals. Often we used a variety of methods to cope. One morning we went into a restaurant just off campus. A waitress came to our table and said she was sorry that they did not serve colored people. A couple of our guys got angry and wanted to turn tables over and leave. I spoke up and told her that I was glad she didn't serve colored people because I didn't want colored people. I wanted ham and eggs. Then we all left. That method is not to say that my dark side from my father's side had not raised up in my spirit. It did so, but I had long since learned that there is a time for everything, and that was not the time for physical violence. To turn tables over was not self-defense. Additionally, I have learned that education was to improve one's ability to solve problems appropriately.

One time we were in the beautiful stadium at North Texas State Relays. The stadium was full, almost like a football game. Bob and I were on the track and setting our blocks for the 100 meter. We had noticed we were the only Afro-Americans in the race. The starter called the runners to stand behind the blocks. Then he said, "Runners take your marks," followed by "Get set," then the gun sounded. One of the white boys jumped, and we were called back. The starter repeated with, "Take your marks," "Get set," and then the gun again. Another jump by a Caucasian boy. A third call back. He repeated it all, and again the gun fired, and a third jump and not from me or Bob. Thinking he was going to call us back, we began to ease up when we heard him say, "Aw, hell, let them run." We played catch up all the way to the 80 yard line. We took first and second, Bob and I respectively.

On the way back up the track, one white boy said to his teammates, "That's the first time I've been beaten by a Negra." It was a southern idiom. Some of our guys who heard it wanted to start something. I asked them to look at the stadium. Of all the people, we saw about five Blacks in the stadium. So I ask them if they could run all the way to Kansas. That brought a laugh and quieted some emotions.

Mel Coates and Bob shared something similar that happened after I had graduated. In spite of all such negatives we encountered, for me it was still better to have been in college. When I compare what we had and the conditions in colleges today, now is a gravy train. I cannot understand why more students do not take advantage where it is available. Especially are community colleges accessible, with grants for lower socioeconomic families.

By the end of my sophomore year I had patched up things with Eligene Clay, the young lady at the church in Kansas City, Kansas. Eligene and I would see each other on many weekends during non-track time. Before I left for college, Eligene's main focus of concern was the care of her mother. My main focus of concern was still how I could get the schooling I so desperately needed. Our separate foci, I believe, caused each of us to question, at least somewhat, whether we were really moving too fast or at least to have some unspoken concerns. Therefore, with our dissimilar concerns, I left for college and Eligene concentrated on helping her mother. I didn't come home for some time, and later found the time apart to have been good for us. By the end of my sophomore year we had refocused and were thinking as one. We would see each other on fewer weekends, especially during my track season. However, we maximized our fewer times together.

As things smoothed out, we began to have plans for marriage. She knew I did not have plans to get married before I graduated. However, the best plans can be interrupted. It so happened that our pastor of Third Street Church of God, Elder Goff David Young and wife, Sister Anna Mae Young, were preparing to take a pastorate in Pasadena, California. This was the fall of my last year. Eligene wanted him to marry us the next summer, 1957. So now I was faced with the question, do I please myself and wait for graduation, or do I please Eligene, whom I loved, and get married before the Youngs left. To risk losing her or risk the degree, since I still had a semester to go. Had she known I was thinking about my degree more, she would have done the easy thing - killed me. So knowing that we did love each other, on December 22, 1956, we heard words like this: "Eligene, do you take this man, Lee Roy Pitts, to be your wedded husband, to have and to cherish, to love and obey in sickness and in health, so long as you both shall live?" Then I heard the same words indicating I was taking on the same intent in the presence of witnesses. We both responded yes, and Elder Young pronounced us man and wife.

We had a simple wedding at the church parsonage. Eligene was given away by her first cousin, Macon Robinson. Her youngest sister, Haroldena Clay, was her maid of honor. My best man was truly my best man, Mr. Arnold Saunders. Before my marriage it was because of him and another friend, Mr. Charles Scott, that I remained with the Third Street Church of God.

Our wedding night was spent in the Townhouse Hotel wedding suite. There are certain things we both remember about the room décor. It brings laughs and smiles when we talk about it from time to time. It is one of those secrets that shall remain forever ours.

Getting married was a good thing for me in many ways. Being married to Eligene was to receive a jewel. At the time I had no way of knowing the many joys that were to come. I could not see the struggles that would also be ours. However, we were ready for some of both. During our courtship we had enough wisdom to discuss and talk about many topics. We shared the pros and cons of our respective families. Such discussions involved things from work habits to how members viewed religion and death. Now I know that even when some of our talk may have been embellished a bit, most of it served us well.

Our own analysis and commitment was all we had in preparation for marriage. We never had premarital counseling, nor heard of such from the ministry at our church. By premarital counseling, I am referring to sessions with a trained minister or professional counselor. I had taken a course titled "Marriage and Family" in college from an excellent professor. I learned about counseling there and found the course very useful. But many, if not most, pastors then and now know very little about the "how" of counseling. However, many of our old ministers would preach such sermons that even without counselors we had enough understanding of the need to commit with Godly intent.

While counseling in our case was lacking, nevertheless we had enough Scriptural foundation that there was in place a prenuptial of the highest. It was written in our hearts. When we said "I do" in the presence of witnesses, we meant to bring it about. We were committed to the belief that any reasons short of Biblical reasons for breaking that bond would not be pleasing to the God we served. Both of us committed to this thinking and to the Biblical purpose of our marriage. That philosophy I called our prenuptial agreement written in our hearts.

After being married and celebrating Christmas, I returned to school in January 1957. The spring of 1957 was the beginning of my senior year. In December of 1957 I was three hours shy of graduation. The summer of 1958, I completed work and received my Bachelor's degree.

When I looked at my degree, I felt like I had accomplished a goal. With proud arrogance I figuratively patted myself on the back. I was humble enough to know I had not climbed Mount Everest, but wise enough to know that I was further up the mountain than I had been. College had equipped me for more than just the work world. My critical thinking and analytical skills had been developed beyond my fondest expectation. Best of all, I was a more internally secure person than when I first walked on the campus of Kansas State Teachers College three years before.

I saw the college evolve from Kansas State Teachers College to Kansas State College to Pittsburg State University. So as my undergraduate days came to an end, I realized that I too had evolved. I was not where I could have been had my upbringing environment been different, or had I been a more mature teenager when I left home. Still, I was not where I had been. Completion of my first degree left me with inexpressible gratitude that has remained with me.

Above all the colleges and universities I have attended, Pittsburg State is and shall remain first in my heart and memory; so grateful am I for what took place within me during my sojourn there.

CHAPTER XII

BEGINNING MY CAREER

Before college but with military Tech Supply and Cartography experience, employment was still difficult. After graduation with a degree in Industrial Engineering Drafting Design and Biology, I was not surprised to find employment yet difficult for me. In reality, while I expected some racial prejudice, I was taken back to find it to be so insidious.

I entered the world of work having been told by Dr. Jack Morgan, my professor of Engineering and Design in Industrial Education, that my portfolio of drawings and designs were among the best he had seen. He left Pittsburg and became a Professor of Engineering at the University of Missouri-Columbia, Missouri. His words of confidence in me stayed with me.

My first exciting possibility for a job came when a company advertised for a beginner design draftsman. I called and spoke with a Mr. Edsell. After a few questions about my background, he told me he definitely would be interested in seeing me. I told him I would be right there. It took me about 30 minutes to arrive at his office. I went up on the elevator to his floor. I stepped off, and there sat a secretary/receptionist who asked if she could help me. I told her my name and that Mr. Edsell was expecting to see me about the design position. She immediately said, "Mr.

Edsell told me to tell all inquirers that the position has been filled." I told her thanks and left. On arriving downstairs in the lobby, I stopped and thought a minute. I went to the telephone and called Mr. Edsell. He answered, and I asked if he was taking applications for the draftsman position. He said yes. I told him I was the gentleman he told to come. He said he was waiting to see me. When I told him that I was there and what his secretary told me, there was silence and a long pause. Finally, I said, "Mr. Edsell, why don't you just tell her to say, 'we do not hire Negroes.'" It seemed to me that he could have detected in my voice who I possibly was racially and have just been honest. The voice technique was often done in those days.

Then there was a time I took my portfolio to a company located on West Gregory in Kansas City, Missouri. The gentlemen, while still looking at my work and turning to the next one, said, "This is good work." I told him thanks. After a few other questions about design, he excused himself for a few minutes. On his return, he told me that he had just discovered that the position was to be filled by an in-house employee. I reached over, closed my portfolio, thanked him for the interview, and left. Procedure would lead me to believe that he would have known beforehand how the position would be filled.

Then I believed that he didn't have the courage to say, "We do not hire Afro-Americans," or "We are not ready to hire Afro-Americans." The sad thing is that I suspect some of those interviewers were just following company policy for their job's sake.

I have not given these examples to drum up racism and segregations past or to cause more hatred. It is mentioned so my grandchildren and great grandchildren will know some of what those before them experienced. They need to know that each generation back experienced far worse conditions. Furthermore, it is my prayer that my grands will see what our children saw. Namely, that with all the obstacles placed in our path, they did not stop us from trying to improve ourselves. Obstacles did not stop us from having behavior that would influence positively the next generation to give them an advantage we did not receive. In our day, even men who hurt daily from the ravages of segregation, who had little hope of things changing, had hope for us. They would tell us to keep going to school and would do whatever it took to help us accomplish that goal. I had no way of knowing that for me the best was yet to come.

Approximately May of 1958 I was approached by the Assistant to the Superintendent, Dr. Bertram Caruthers. He told me about an opening for a teacher of General Science. The requirement was for a science major. I applied for the position and placed his name and Daniel Webster Lewis, a Secondary Supervisor, as persons who could be contacted for a character reference. Dr. Caruthers had taught me freshman science in the same room that if hired, I would be teaching. Mr. Lewis was my elementary principal at Grant Elementary School. He knew my aunt who raised me and years later would ask me how Mrs. Love was faring. I was interviewed for the position, and several weeks later I received a contract. With my son about five months old, needless to say, I accepted the position as the new science teacher.

I had written a number of applications and had a number of interviews. Only one resulted in a job offer. Boeing Aircraft in Wichita, Kansas, offered me an engineering drafting and design position. It came after I had accepted the teaching position. A short time later I read that Boeing was laying off and on strike.

In the fall of 1958, a teaching career that was to last fifty years was started. Before that I had no plans to teach, let alone to remain in the field for so many years. Aunt Lydia was happy to know I was a teacher, though she had no idea how I became one. From the very beginning Eligene was supportive of my plans. She had taken a chance with me after learning that I had not completed high school. Under similar circumstances I wouldn't have recommended that my daughter get serious with someone with my background before seeing his track record more closely. Now with my contract, she too was excited, as we as a team embarked on our first job since getting married.

My first year class was exceptional in many ways: athletics, intellectually, and social relations. They were so good academically and I was so green as a new teacher, that many years afterwards I wished I could have had them later in my career. In many respects they were teaching me. Then there were the parents of these wonderful students. During our annual open house the parents wanted to know how their respective child was doing. Equally they wanted to know what they could do to help me. Always they were supportive of my plans for the year, plans such as field trips and work projects.

A number of my students were children of my former teachers. Some of my teachers were still at Northeast during my early years. So in one sense that could have been very tense for me. However, the very opposite was true - those children were some of the most helpful.

Because I had such high regard for my teachers, it was difficult to adjust to being a teacher. I do not recall when I accepted the fact emotionally. Things just took their natural course with all of us busy teaching, learning our students, their names and behavior. After a while I was simply too busy to be tense.

My biggest trial came on the first day. I knew the students were going to challenge my authority in some way. In military service I learned that I was "out of order" if I couldn't keep order. The first students that entered were in what was called their "homeroom" class. It was there they would go first each day, and they would leave from there each evening for home. Their coats would remain in that room each day.

Things had not changed since my student days. They had selected a boy to be the challenger. So when I said, "Please get in your seats," all sat except him. He remained standing in the rear of the room directly opposite from where I was standing. It became quiet as both sides turned inward watching him, then me. I stared at him and in a quiet tone said, "I said, get in your seats." He remained standing.

I removed my glasses, placed them on my desk, and with my military sergeant voice said, "I told you to get in your seat, and if you do not, I will come and help you get in it." All the while I was thinking, "Lord, help this kid to sit down." I started to the back with my gaze on him, and before I got halfway, he slowly slid into his seat. Of note is this young man was one of my finest students behaviorally. As with many in that class, we are still very good friends.

Out of that class came a number of professionals. There were medical doctors, an architect, accountants, educators, nurses, ministers, tradesmen, and self-employed business persons. I did not know what to expect, but I thought having so many gifted students in one class was unusual. I recall asking Mr. William Boone, our principal, how often I would get a class like that one. He told me about every three years. Some five or so years later I told him I was still waiting. He and I both laughed. I discovered that in every class, every year there were some bright students. Some years there are more and other years less.

My wife says that I talked about my first year class more than any other. She says it is my favorite. It is true that they lead the many students I have had, college included, in gift-edness. However, my experience at Northeast causes many students to be special, first year and other years. I will never forget many of them. The names Watson, M.D.; Caruthers, M.D.; Favors, M.D.; Porter, R.N.; Owens, accountant; Bradley, musician; Thierry, opera; Stevens, architect; Welch, Ph.D.; Buford, educator; Foggs, educator; Young, minister; Foggs, M.D., J. E. Young, Ph.D., O. Taylor, M.D., and a number of others come to mind when I think of Northeast.

Without doubt I got spoiled with my first year class. I could not have started teaching with a better group. When I think of the opportunity and privilege that was mine to be involved with a wide array of students I am aware of the growth that was mine also.

Some of our students left Sumner for some of the best universities in the world. James Lindesay - MIT, Ph.D., Physics; Walter Rice - Astrophysics, Ph.D.; Michael Foggs - Yale, Harvard, M.D.; Toni Peeler - Northwestern, Howard University, M.D.; Linda Boone - Kansas University, Ph.D., and a number of others that I didn't have in my science class.

The Northeast Junior/Sumner High School complex was a powerhouse with parents, students, and teachers of the highest caliber. For fate to have allowed me to be a part of it often brings an indescribable emotional high when I think about it.

During all of my years of teaching, my wife and I were a team. On more than a few occasions students would stop by, and Eligene would feed them. I have never been deserving of the kind of support I have received from her. When I became the head track coach, I learned that one of my boys was hungry. I went to his house, and his mother said her husband had not been home for days and she had little money. She had purchased marshmallows and milk to keep them from getting hungry. Other than the boy on the track team, the children all looked to be less than eight years of age and five in number.

I got the telephone number and name of our church Secretary, Mrs. Shirley Lewis of the Third Street Church of God. I told her they would see that her family received food and the guidance she needed for future help. I took her 15-year-old son home and told my wife he was hungry. He ate so fast that our son Eric was so moved watching him that he went into another room and emotionally said, "Daddy, he is really hungry." It was an opportunity for our children to know that even though we were not rich, we lived with the mandate to help the less fortunate.

As I stated, so many times at Northeast we had a diverse student population. There were students whose parents were college graduates, those without college, children of professionals - doctors, lawyers - and children of tradesmen. Some parents had good jobs while some were jobless. So economically we had the well off to those who were daily in need of all kinds of help and so received government assistance.

There I stood those first years, still with regrets of not having completed high school with my Sumner class. When I stood looking at the students and then in retrospect thought of my early home life, it was the oddest feeling that somehow I had been prepared to be there. While I never intentionally slighted any students, I did intentionally take notice of those who needed help the most. Then I spent what to some would be an inordinate amount of time helping those in greatest need. Sometimes the help was over academic work; other times a student needed me to listen. Listening and watching student responses often were helpful in deciding if the concern warranted sending a student to our counselors. It didn't take long to see that a combination of things could be helpful in helping students. Another great help was the interaction of younger teachers with older, more seasoned ones.

At Northeast we had a mix of teachers. Many of the women had little to no experience in the streets. On the other hand, we had some men who had street smarts enough to better handle the few students with too much street experience for their age. This mix of teacher backgrounds gave us uncommon abilities to relate to our diverse population. It was a badge of pride when we could see positive accomplishment and improvement in students because of teamwork. We referred, consulted with each other, and shared ideas on how to best handle situations. We taught, tested, reached out, listened, encouraged students, and did whatever was required to help students. I know of no teachers who habitually left school on time each day. Some of what was done to help students would be looked upon as exceeding reasonable limits by many people in other professions. For us, it was all in a day's work.

Actually we were doing what so many of us experienced with teachers in the segregated all-Black schools from which we had all come. After integration, we received Caucasian teachers, most of whom were at odds initially, but soon fit in wonderfully. Those who fit in were those who wanted to be there at Northeast. We jelled into a strong team and proved that regardless of ethnicity, a good teacher can teach children.

In the early stages of integration we noticed that we received a few teachers who did not want to be with us, as well as Black teachers who did not want to transfer. In time, much of that smoothed out, and like my personal children, children were taught by good teachers, Black and white. Students, like adults, have their favorites, and it does not have to be about color.

There are a few students who state they experienced favoritism at Northeast and Sumner High. One upperclassmen during my student days believed that children of teachers and well known community leaders were favored over other students. While that may have been true in some instances, from my perspective, it was definitely not the norm. I am speaking from years of working with teachers at Northeast and involvement with the math and science teachers at Sumner High School.

After teaching at the community college with its array of teachers, I know that our faculty at Northeast was not only academically qualified but superior to most in regard to delivery of subject matter and modes of delivery. I recall some outcomes of teaching such as exams and other means of determining competence that occurred at Northeast. All of it speaks to the caliber of our teaching at Northeast and Sumner High School.

The Greater Kansas City Science Fair was a big thing, just as in other cities. My first year I had one student who entered the fair. He was Myles Stevens, son of a prominent attorney and a mother who taught at Sumner High School. Myles won first place in the physical science division, junior high section. He went on to Sumner High School, then college, where he became an architect. Veda Monday won her division in the Science Fair and continues today to help other students in the community to excel.

Also I had two students who won their division, and in both cases the science fair leader questioned if a freshman could do that level of work. Our principal, Mr. Boone, wrote a letter testifying that they had done the work. One of the students was Walter Rice and the other was James Lindesay. Both of them went on to Sumner High School and repeated the success under a brilliant math and physics teacher named Mr. William Smith. Both of them went on to receive Ph.D.s in Physics at Harvard and MIT.

Several other examples of the outcome of our teaching come to mind. Two of our Industrial Arts teachers, Mr. Webster McGee and Mr. William Walker, took students with their projects to the state industrial arts program, and there, also, suggestions were made that junior high school students could not do that kind of shop work. These types of statements became a joke for our faculty, because we knew we had boys in shop who, figuratively, could make you a suit of clothes with a piece of wood. Additionally, we knew we had students who were equally as good in English, journalism, music - vocal, and instrumental - and often were perceived by visitors as high school students rather than junior high.

During my first years of teaching, I knew that all of our students would be continuing at Sumner High. Segregation was on, and that was the only school for Black students. I knew that we were preparing students to meet an excellent faculty, some of whom were still there from my student days. Knowing this to be true gave me personal pride to be part of the success of Sumner High School. Some of the success at Sumner was due to what had been taught at

Northeast. Likewise, the students we received had been given a foundation on which we could build. The foundation was given by some important, if not the most important teachers - the elementary school teachers.

Just as I speak fondly of my teachers, it has been a pleasure to hear my own children speak about their teachers, some of whom were my colleagues and some my former teachers. Recently, I asked Gina, our daughter, a question about what was preferred in English grammar and how she knew what was correct. It was her delight to tell me what was correct. However, it was a greater delight to put me in my place by telling me she knows because Mrs. Marjorie Rhone said thus and so, and that is why it is correct - now. Mrs. Rhone was a colleague at Northeast. She went on to teach at high school, and Gina was under her there. For one reason or the other - all positive reasons - I have heard other names around our house. The names of Freeman Crawford, Mercelyn Gilbert, John Henson, Lee J. Lindsay, Harold Foster, Melgin Williams, Patricia Caruthers, John Rice, Carol Hams, Melvin Smith, Melba Hall, John Henderson, Mr. Lawrence, Edward Eddy, and Wanda Miller, to name a few.

As we sat at dinner listening to our children speak about their teachers, I realized these teachers gave more than subject matter. I felt personally indebted to that cadre of teachers and have told them so many times.

Contractually teachers are hired to teach subject matter. However, most teachers find it needful to do other, often and more likely, nonpaying tasks. My experience was no different. However, in my case, some of the tasks I took on had their inception with something I experienced in college.

When I was in college, slide rules were being used in a number of disciplines, particularly math and science courses. I recall being in engineering drawing class and physics, where many had this instrument hanging on their belt when not in use. I was told they had learned how to use it in high school. It was then that I formed my own opinion about why some students have advantages over others. I started emphasizing IQ less because I started believing that, with some exceptions, most of us have enough IQ to learn most of what we need in order to function in life. I started stressing exposure as being most important to our children, as it was for me in college classes.

It was with that in mind that I started a program to expose my science students to anything technical that I thought would help them in science while with me and after they got to Sumner High School. Each year I took a bus load of students to the University of Kansas in Lawrence for Science and Math Day. Several years I took two buses. Always I received volunteer help from the other science and math teachers. I began taking smaller groups to the internationally known Linda Hall Science Library located in Kansas City, Missouri. There they were introduced to the program offerings of that library. They learned the what and how of Bioabstracts. Most of my students enjoyed the exposure and more than a few understood how valuable the exposure was.

Seeking to combine talent with needs, I started a program to get jobs for students that would expose them to some area of science. My personal physician was Dr. A. P. Taliaferro. His clinic was at 13th and Waverly, two blocks from our house. One evening I went down and spoke with him about wanting to expose children by placing them in jobs around professionals. First it would satisfy a need of families while helping my students to become comfortable around professionals. Dr. T, as we called him, took to the idea with as much excitement as I had, then added his input. He suggested that he would take a boy and start him with simple tasks and begin working with him on more complicated work as he learned.

The first student I had in mind was an academically talented and focused young man from a very good family. As I recall, his father was ill at the time. He was Michael Foggs. Michael worked there after he left my class and throughout his Sumner High School years. He attended Yale University undergrad and Harvard Medical School, where he graduated with highest honors. He is now one of the top immunologists in the country.

Following Michael I placed a boy named Allen Garrett in Dr. T's office. Allen, like Michael, was academically talented and in need financially. He stayed there all three years while a student at Sumner High. He also went on to receive his M.D. degree.

I am glad to say for some twelve years before leaving secondary teaching, I placed students in both doctors' and pharmacists' offices. Now such programs are funded by outside sourcing or government grants. Back then Dr. Taliaferro was picking up the tab and contributing to the education of young people. He had a way of asking questions that was helpful to those students. We were actually ministering to needs of young people. Dr. Taliaferro, like myself, saw immediately the need and how he could help satisfy the need, at least in part.

While I was trying to expose them to technical areas and science, the teachings of Jesus were ever on my mind. Jesus gave us the idea that some people need a physician the most. Also the thoughts of the late Mother Teresa come to mind. One day her workers were feeding the poor, and she remarked, "Feed the poorest of the poor first." I'm not saying these students I selected were the poorest, but I know my reality indicated there was great need.

We were an urban, all Afro-American school, which is an indication of the types of needs of our children. Just as I selected an area to help, almost all of our teachers were going the extra mile to help students in some non-contractual manner. If you were there, it did not take long to see the need and wish you could help more. In my opinion, many teachers elsewhere were committed to students. However, during those years of segregation, with less concern for our students from the larger society, commitment from the teachers at Northeast and Sumner was not a choice but a necessity. We had to think futuristically in regard to our children.

A few years after Michael Foggs headed to Yale University, our son Eric Wayne went there. I will never forget something he said to me. He said, "Daddy, I have a number of classmates from Northeast and Sumner High who would have done well here at Yale."

When my two oldest children became teenagers, I was in my last year of teaching at Northeast Junior before going on to teach at community college. By then, other programs began to be available and financed by local and Federal grants, so whereas my own children were not involved in the program I started, they did enter a newer program called Health Careers. As I recall, a number of our local Black medical doctors gave this program the guidance for its success. Our son Eric Wayne and our daughter Gina were two of a number of students in the program. The doctors kept the program with the intent, namely, to increase student success in the field of medicine. The success of that program substantiates my claim that exposure is the key to improvement.

One contribution to education of which I am most proud had its inception around my third year of teaching. One evening, one of my finest students academically and behaviorally, asked to speak with me. She told me she was pregnant by a young boy who also was in my class. I suggested she see one of our counselors that evening or the next day. Her mother had been told, but not her father, which was the cause of much anxiety in her. She was the daughter of a wonderful mom and dad that I knew personally. Her dad was a minister of the gospel.

I went home that evening and shared it with my wife without telling her all the details. Because I knew there were no programs to keep these girls in school and, coupled with knowing her ability, I found myself emotionally moved before lying down for the night. I suspect that some of my hurt was recalling what I went through when I left school and now transferring those feelings to her. Eventually I told Eligene what was bothering me. Whatever the cause for my being upset, I was disgusted by the system not allowing girls like her a way to continue.

After sleeping awhile, I woke with thoughts for a seminar to avert teen pregnancies. I immediately got up, got paper and pencil, and began to write. The next morning I organized my notes into a program around teen sexuality. The Director of Black Adoption, Inc., learned of my seminar, and soon I was presenting it in schools for them. One principal of our sister school, Northwest Junior, told me that since my seminar had been presented, his pregnancies were cut in half in three years. Mr. Brown reiterated that several times to me.

Soon I was using the seminar on behalf of my fraternity, Alpha Phi Alpha, and various churches. Now fifty years since starting the seminar, I am still presenting it wherever the opportunity is available in the metro area. I enjoy giving the seminar because it is an opportunity to expose youth to other ways of seeing and thinking about their sexuality.

Many of the teens I worked with have never been exposed to sound rational thinking. However, the majority will often exhibit rational thought when exposed to certain situations. Much can be accomplished when working one-on-one or with small groups. However, in group settings, teens often show behavior just to get laughs, such as making fun of each other or talking about each other's relatives. Such behavior is said to be indicative of the "Damaged Cargo Syndrome." This syndrome is when one speaks of behavior that is a result often of minority African American history of the middle passage, slavery, Jim Crow, and second class citizenship. Much of that resulted in people being disconnected from better thinking of who they are in their value (Lanney, 2006, 25).

The title of my teen sexuality seminars is "Remember your ABC's." I attempt to drill into participants' minds that all Belief leads to Action, and all Action has a Consequence. I found that too often the young do not look at all behavior as assets or liabilities. How they look, speak, and relate is seldom translated or questioned as to whether it is an asset to what they want to accomplish or a liability or hindrance.

When I presented the seminar as part of my fraternity's national emphasis on teen sexuality, we had good success. Some success was determined by giving pre and post tests and checking responses. We tried to expose boys to thinking in ways that give advantage in whatever situation the boys found themselves. Sometimes it requires sacrificial action to be beneficial.

I recall a sacrificial action that was a learning situation for my own preteen children. One Friday night Michael

Foggs stopped by our house at 1038 Waverly. He was on his way to Dr. Taliaferro's at 13th and Waverly. I asked him if he was going to the football game, and he said, "No." So the football game was on, but Mike was on his way to work. I was glad my children heard him, because they learned from someone they knew personally that often sacrifice is the need. They were seeing in Michael's action what they would later read in a book by M. Scott Peck, M.D. titled The Road Less Traveled. In it, Peck states that the inability to delay gratification can create problems in many areas of life, but some 15- or 16-year-olds have hardly developed the capacity (Peck, 1978, 20).

Thinking about sacrifice, another contributing factor to our success at Northeast comes to mind. I am thinking about our counseling program. It was headed by Mr. Jackson C. VanTrece and his coworker, Mrs. Josephine Vandiver (now Boone). I would be less than truthful if I did not say it is my opinion that these two were the best counselors in our school district. I speak of their intellectual capability and academic preparation. They did the usual for counselors: listened to student concerns, placed students in courses, and gave required state tests. Then I know they went beyond the required. I am aware that they gave special attention to physically challenged student needs, placing them in electives that would increase their success in high school. Both of these people worked to get each student involved in at least one school activity. They would help students to feel a sense of belonging. Being excellent teachers themselves, they were able to help teachers with help for special needs children as well.

Mr. VanTrece did not always go straight home in the evening. He went to a Community Center program in which activities for youth were ongoing. Many young men today testify that if it had not been for Mr. VanTrece at the evening program, they do not know what would have become of them.

Jackson VanTrece and I met when I was still working on my Bachelor's degree. I was taking a class in the summer semester and he was at Pittsburg State for work in counseling while working full time as a counselor at Northeast Junior High in Kansas City, Kansas. I had no plans to enter the ranks of teaching. My meeting Jackson Van Trece and seeing how things evolved to the friendship we have today is not only interesting but for some, it would be seen as mystical.

That summer I caught a ride home with Jackson VanTrece and another Northeast teacher named James C. Lyons. I sat in the back and listened to their talk. From Pittsburg, Kansas, to Kansas City, Kansas, they talked about life at Northeast. Life with the principal, teachers, and students. Not just broad issues did they talk about, but some specifics. Little did I know that the non-confidential issues of which they spoke were really like a preparatory talk to me as a beginning teacher. I rode with them a number of times during those summers. I was surprised how helpful that was to me when I began to work at Northeast.

Mr. Jackson VanTrece is still one of the finest men whom I have encountered. He was of great personal help to me when I was teaching. His wife Dorothy and my wife Eligene worked together and became good friends. Jack, as we often called him, soon was transferred to a high school as Vice Principal, and I replaced him as counselor at Northeast Junior High.

It was then my pleasure to work with and under the leadership of Mrs. Josephine Vandiver, who was Head Counselor. It was then that I got a chance to know how sharp was her mind and her concern for youth. I had taken courses at Central Missouri State University in Warrensburg, Missouri, and was a certified school counselor. However, there was nothing equal to what I learned as I sat across from this lady while discussing matters involving some of our respective clientele. Many were the times I would hear her words but more importantly, the spirit and character behind them as seen in her quiet demeanor and concern for some child who was a target of an unjust act. Because of the manner in which she carried herself, I still call her, with affection, Lady Vandiver. When she hears it, she knows it is one of only two who call her that with fondness, me and the late Dr. Andrew Stevenson, former President of Penn Valley College and my college roommate.

As I said, Mr. VanTrece and Lady Vandiver contributed much to our success. The depth of their commitment was seen when they made information available to keep us reminded of the width of our students' abilities and needs. It was such a pleasure to have met and worked with them.

Most of the teachers at Northeast went on to do graduate work and received degrees in their field. I joined the trend by attending the University of Colorado at Boulder for two summers on a National Science Foundation grant. There I took graduate Chemistry, Physics, and Biology courses. I received an opportunity there that few who attend small colleges experience. I was taught by a Nobel Laureate and world renown cosmologist and physicist - Dr. George Gamow. I was not alone in being awestruck to hear him call Einstein, Enrico Fermi, and other well known great scientists by their first names. Afterwards, a number of us were saying, "Did you hear him say 'Albert said such and such,' when speaking of Albert Einstein?" It was under this professor that for the first time I understood Albert Einstein's

Theory of Relativity.

I returned to Pittsburg State for study and received my Master's degree in Biology in 1967.

In 1970 I left Northeast Junior High School, but the experience remains with me to this day. I left, but the teachers and students there remain second to no other teachers and students.

It is fitting to close talk about my experiences at Northeast Junior High by saying something about the teacher who was the influence behind my attending Pittsburg State University. I speak of none other than Mrs. Rozella K. Caldwell-Swisher. In my student days she was called Miss Caldwell, my Social Studies teacher. I am not sure at that time which we liked more, her always beautifully decorated room or her. She was a very good looking, excitable, high energy, slightly Indian-looking Afro-American.

She and her husband Lawrence had attended Kansas State Teachers College, now Pittsburg State University, in the 1930s. He was a track star and personally knew the notable Jesse Owens, since Pittsburg was nationally known in track and field. Mr. Swisher often visited the school during the summer semesters, and since I was on the track team I got to know him during those summers. So when I went to work at Northeast, I had already met Miss Caldwell's husband. She didn't know I was going to teach, and was surprised but glad to welcome me into the profession.

I remember when I was a student in her class we had to keep a scrapbook of current events. I did not like keeping a scrapbook. I thought it took too much of my time, and I did not see the benefit of the assignment. However, I did keep the book because you could get extra credit. One boy placed a pretty flower on the front of his book and received extra credit. I creatively used match sticks to form words for the front cover of my book. I removed the match heads, colored the sticks, and pasted them onto the front. I did not receive extra credit, and when I discovered later that both of us had the required items inside, I got angry. My anger wasn't for long, because there was too much work and too many interesting things to do to stay angry. While I recall that one incident, greater still are the positives of her class that have stayed in my memory over the years.

Some days when we would get finished with certain assignments, she would say, "You may go to the library and read for broader knowledge." It was a simple statement back then, but later it took on real meaning. She put reading on our minds. Whether or not we took the time to do so was our choice. Today I am actually uncomfortable without a book to read. Especially is this so when I am in places where I have to wait for considerable periods of time. I have a belief that it was started with her emphasis on "reading for broader knowledge."

Often she shared with us about her travel to other places. What she shared fit in well with articles we read in a periodical called "The Weekly Reader." The articles were made more meaningful because of her reports of travel. I think it caused our minds to momentarily soar to other places. While I remembered those positives about Miss Caldwell, the one that was most important to me was her talk about going to school in Pittsburg, Kansas. Ultimately, I went to Pittsburg because I remembered that she had gone there.

When I went to work at Northeast I thought I knew Miss Caldwell. Little did I know that I would soon really get to know this Grand Lady. Starting with my first year there, I was to learn and come to understand the inner workings of a great teacher's mind, as I spent time with her one-on-one and in group sessions. Soon I began stopping by her room after school and asking her, How is the Grand Lady of Northeast doing? She knew that privately I addressed her in that manner, out of my respect and esteem for her. She would invite me in and the wisdom lesson, like the wisdom from mother to son, would begin to flow. It was during such talks that I learned how little I had known about her during my student days. Listening and watching her gave me a head start on being a success at Northeast and teaching in general.

I remember my first day at Northeast and what she told me upon seeing me. She greeted me with a big smile and an extended handshake. Then she said, "LaRoy, if you teach at Northeast for one year, you will be able to teach anywhere." She always pronounced my name as if it was spelled "LaRoy," rather than Lee Roy. To this day, my oldest friend, Bill, will call me, mimicking Miss Caldwell, and say he wants to speak with "LaRoy." I can tell from his voice that he is grinning. I must add that he also liked Miss Caldwell and we were in her class, same subject, same hour.

By the time I went to work at Northeast she began using her married name and was Mrs. Swisher. It was not long before I believed that by any standard Mrs. Swisher was one of the wisest persons I had known. If need be, she could wear a number of different hats and wear them with finesse and brilliance. Many were the times I saw her act as Social Studies teacher, arguing for her students, but I also saw her at community meetings wearing the hat of religious leader.

Mrs. Swisher could out-strategize or out-plan the best of persons. Coupled with how to plan, she also knew tactics. That is, once having her plan, she could then execute the necessary maneuvers to accomplish her goal. What I learned in the military about Strategy and Tactics had nothing on this Master Teacher.

This Master could hold her own in any educational argument or debate regarding students. I know very few arguments during faculty or district meetings in which she did not come out on top. Consequently, when we wanted to get something or do something that was likely to be rejected by the principal, Mr. William Boone, we got Mrs. Swisher to push it. In private I told her that had she been a Caucasian woman, she would be in the White House. To that she would give me that Caldwell smile and say something about what she did was for her "Junior Citizens." That's the way she referred to her students.

As time went on, I continued to be impressed by her. I found her to be more congruent than many, if not most people. That is, she was not hypocritical. Her speech about topics matched her actions. I never found her speaking one thing in faculty meetings or being silent, then later talk about what should have been. She was forthright and would not hedge on what she believed was right.

As a new teacher, I learned things about planning that short circuited many failures that would have been mine without her wisdom. She impacted my life in the area of planning and her conscious awareness of the God from where her gifts came.

During our generation as students we were fortunate. Fortunate, because to my knowledge, from elementary to high school, our teachers believed in God. They believed in planning and hard work, but also in prayer to help bring their hard work to success. I recall that all of our special programs like the Honor Society, started with something to acknowledge God. We knew whatever the program, usually, somewhere behind it would be our strong Master teachers, Miss Mattie Williams and her dear friend and colleague, Rozella Caldwell-Swisher.

When Jesse Owens visited Sumner High School, it was Miss Caldwell who introduced me to him. She called me and said, "LaRoy, we are going to Sumner tomorrow." She told the principal she was going and was taking me with her. Mr. Boone took care of our classes. That was the work of my teacher, Mrs. Rozella K. Caldwell-Swisher. In a recent reunion of Afro-Americans who attended Pittsburg State University, her name was called in honor of her labors among us.

CHAPTER XIII

WRAPPING UP MY CAREER

My final teaching contract assignment came when I was talking with my friend and college roommate, Andrew Victor Stevenson. Word had been floating that Northeast Junior High would soon be closed and faculty would be integrated into other schools. Integration had already begun, and we had worked with wonderful Caucasian teachers with no problems. With my upbringing in the West Bottoms and the military, working with other ethnic groups never came to mind as being a possible problem. Very few teachers were concerned about integration, but virtually all teachers, Black and white, were concerned about the administrative policies and procedures to implement the process. As with most other places in the nation, integration was successful in the district.

Meanwhile, while all the talk of closing Northeast was circulating, I did not know that Penn Valley Community College in Kansas City, Missouri, wanted to bring more minorities on board in all areas. Andrew was Dean of Students there, so he was aware of both the college's wants and the procedures that outsiders needed to know to make application.

He spoke with the then head of the Biology department about me needing a job and that I was a good teacher. The chairperson was Dr. Dolores Meyers. Dr. Meyers called me and said, "I heard you were a good teacher and needed a job." I told her the latter was true, but I didn't know about the former and that I worked toward being good. She asked me if I could bring a transcript and come to see her.

When I went to see her the school was located at the old Westport Road campus. She looked at my transcript and said I was fine and mentioned what I would be teaching if hired. Then our conversation drifted into areas wherein she could get to know me. After talking about my experiences in Kansas and feeling comfortable, somehow the question surfaced as to whether I was a Christian. Both of us were aware that such questions were off limits or were supposed to be during a job interview. By then both of us must have felt comfortable, or the question would not have surfaced. All the while during the asking, I remember she had a smile as she also let me know I didn't have to answer that question. To the question I told her I was. Then again with a smile she said, "Practicing?" to which I asked, "Is there any other?" She laughed and said, "I'm going to like you." After meeting with a dean and several other committee members, I got the job.

When I first started there, I recall only one person in Biology who overtly acted uncomfortable with my presence. If others had similar feelings, I didn't know about it. I received much help to assist my transition to college procedures and policies. It was not long before I had many wonderful friends and felt like being there was like my second home. I remained with Metropolitan Community College District, specifically assigned to Penn Valley Community College, for thirty-five years, twenty-five fulltime and ten years part-time retired.

I was officially a faculty member of Penn Valley Community College. It was a community college and according to Munroe, "Such colleges were becoming the fastest expanding segment of public education. Such colleges were increasingly becoming the answer to the question: 'Shall I or shall I not go to college?' The goal to maximize educational opportunities for all, the rich and the poor, the young and the old, was manifested in the development of the public community college" (Munroe, Profile of the Community College, 3).

My secondary teaching, my personality, and my teaching style equipped me well for what was expected of the community college teacher. "The community college teacher was expected to be student oriented although most at the time were subject-matter oriented. They were to accept and gladly work with students of an extraordinary range of abilities and motivations, ranging from the obviously-doomed-to-flunk student, who entered the community college for lack of anything better to do, to the occasionally very bright and even brilliant student who, for reasons of his own, chose to begin his collegiate career in the local public college" (Munroe, Profile of the Community College, 3).

Teaching at Penn Valley College was one of the most satisfying experiences I've had. I also served a stint as chairperson of the Biology department. At the college we taught all levels of students. I taught students who struggled to get out of college and some who had degrees from law schools and schools like Annapolis Naval Academy. Often such latter students were in need of Biology or Zoology before heading to dental school or medical school.

When I retired, there were many new faces in the department, and the department was still, in my opinion, one of the best in the metro area. While at Penn Valley I made some of the finest friends in every department. Some of them I will never forget. I will refrain from listing names of those special ones, but I am sure they not only know of whom I speak but how I feel about them.

In the movie Patton there was a scene where General Patton, speaking of war, says, "I love it more than my life." When I look back on my life there are three things I have loved more than my life.

One of them is my occupation of teaching. I taught for virtually fifty years, full and part time together. I had not planned on teaching when I entered college; however, looking back, I now believe the profession was best for me. I had grown up at a time when poor people were taking care of daily needs with little time for believing it would or could be any different. When I began teaching we had students from such backgrounds. We also had those from well-to-do families. Things were not too different from when I was a student there. Many of us back then also found many obstacles to learning. How I remember being ashamed to eat my peanut butter and biscuit sandwich in the cafeteria! I never had money to eat in the cafeteria, so I carried my lunch so my sisters could eat in the cafeteria. Bill Sappington and I were usually in similar circumstances regarding lunches.

After starting to teach, it was not long before I realized that my background meshed with the daily struggle and outlook of many of my students. From this observation I developed my philosophy of teaching which is: "Our battle is to get our youth to believe in their possibility and in the worth of trying."

I carried this philosophy to college teaching when I left secondary teaching. There, as in secondary teaching, I found that most learning problems could be overcome if I could get students to believe they could, then believe it was worth a try.

It became a challenge for close to fifty years that I loved more than life itself. I remain grateful for the opportunity of teaching. I have other talents and skills, but few could have given me the satisfaction I derived from teaching. Personally, I think many teachers love teaching more than life. It is as if we were chosen in the womb.

CHAPTER XIV

THE JOYS OF BEING MARRIED

The best of my life began when I married Eligene Clay. I brought to the marriage the early influence of some family members. I had a number of cousins on my mother's side and a number of older sisters on my father's side. But it was only a few members whose presence I was in enough to be influenced by their behavior, words, and outlook. It was their influence that I carried with me when I left home.

The oldest members on my mother's side that I knew or knew about were my grandfather, Thomas Lockridge, and his two sisters, our great aunts, Rebecca Vincson and Lydia Swain. My grandfather, who died a month before I was born, had a number of children of whom my mother - Charlotte - was the youngest. Thomas was next oldest. Continuing upwards to the oldest was Aunt Martha Burkehead, Uncle Alfred, and Aunt Lydia Love.

There were other cousins that we knew and some we discovered after I was an adult. Cousin Willa Frances' family we knew well, but only saw them infrequently and so did not feel their influence.

On my dad's side the same was true. I was not around any of them enough. Therefore I was not influenced by any of their ideas and views of life. This is true for my dad as well.

Regrettably, I was not around our great Aunt Rebecca often, but she always came when someone was very sick and nearing death. One positive about her was she knew us by name when she saw us. Always - I repeat, always - she was encouraging. I remember her usual question was, are you in school? If not, why?

It was my Aunt Lydia, Aunt Martha, and Uncle Alfred and their children that I was around on a daily or weekly basis. Aunt Martha always gave each of us something on our birthday as well as Christmas. If she didn't come, then one of her children would bring our presents. Often she came just to see "Sis," as she affectionately called Aunt Lydia. Her husband, John Burkehead, was another uncle that I loved. Many times we visited his house with Aunt Lydia. I would then get a chance to go around Fifth Street and Seventh Street with my cousin, Melvin Burkehead.

For me and my brother Albert, Uncle Alfred and his oldest son Emmitt were good for us. It was from them and my brother that I learned many things that boys need in order to develop into manhood and to survive. I felt comfortable talking with them about most things. Both Aunt Lydia and Aunt Martha knew how to survive, but my Uncle Alfred and cousin Emmitt talked to me with the masculine perspective. That was something I needed to make it in the streets in the Bottoms with the diverse people therein.

One thing I noticed about all of my mom's side of my family was they all believed in going to church. We had to go to church somewhere. I am sure this was the influence of my grandfather, Thomas Lockridge, and possibly my great grandfather, Robert Lockridge. All of my aunts loved my grandfather, their daddy or poppa, as they called him.

None of my uncles or aunts were highly educated. To my knowledge, none had been exposed to many of the philosophical concepts we normally receive in college. But somewhere along the way they had an experience that caused them to believe that if you did unto others the way you wanted them to do unto you, somehow you would have an internal peace for practicing that view. They believed their God hated evil. They followed the tenets of the Hebrew-Christian Bible and believed it was their Holy Book and therefore their rule of conduct. When things got tough, I can't tell how many times I heard my aunt say, "God will take care of us." I mention all of these people because they were my foundation family members.

When I quit high school and left home, I had been exposed to three of my foundation family members more than any others. They were my Uncle Alfred, Aunt Martha, and Aunt Lydia. I had to take all I received from them, and interpret and apply it for myself as I moved through my new experiences. Since I left home as a teenager, what I had to do was a tall order. However, I was ahead of my foundation family. Virtually all of them were on their own before sixteen years of age and facing a much more rugged world.

Now as a senior I see more clearly how much I received from them. How different my life would be were it not for many essentials for life that I received from them. When I consider that my folks were living their lives carrying weights, some of which were due to a segregated world, I marvel at their ability to maintain internal peace and focus in spite of the obstacles faced. Their task was to take me and four other siblings and create an environment for our growth and development. During my teen years, which usually means immature youth, sometimes headstrong, they had to keep me from succumbing to the destructive elements in our neighborhood and keep me in the middle of the road. I think they did an exceptional job.

However, my Aunt Lydia who raised me surpasses them all. After all, it was she and her husband, Isom Love, who took us five children into their home when momma died. Though he and I did not have the best relations in my latter teen years, at least I lived in his house for eleven years starting at age five. I never felt insecure from outside sources, and I was aware of the benefits of his hard work. For all of that I am grateful. All that I learned from the above people served as my preparatory course for marriage and just about all else that I did.

When I was a youngster, I often heard the popular saying, "I have been wrong so long but I am so right tonight." That saying is very applicable to the night of December 22, 1956, the night of my marriage to Eligene Clay. For some time up to then my normal hormonal levels had been trying to override my need for schooling and had lost out. I had plans to get married and attend college with Eligene. She had other plans. One of us was wrong at the time. Hers was for a good cause, as was mine. But having spent much time together getting to know each other, I think on the night we said, "I do," it can be said that we may have been wrong so long but we were so right on that night.

We were far less than rich, monetarily. However, we had each other and a short track record that showed both of us had already faced and conquered hardships. So according to our track record and mindset, we thought we were ready and that the best was yet to come.

So we stood before Elder Goff Young and his wife and pledged to each other our Troth. This was and remains the strength of our marriage. In Doctor Robert Noble's class of Marriage and Family at Pittsburg State University, I learned that "troth" is an old English term that involves loyalty, trust, love, devotion, and reliability. When we pledged this, it meant that from then on Eligene could count on me and I her. So our journey began.

I married a girl I first saw when she was something like six or seven years of age. That view quickly faded from memory. However, when I was on military furlough at eighteen years of age, I saw a girl with hair in bangs, long legs, a big smile, and personable. That view has not faded from my memory.

Growing up, both of us had experienced things in our families that we thought should have been and could have been different. I having had a father that was absent and Eligene a father who was sometimes there and sometimes not, we were determined to do better. Before marriage we were aware that we were dreaming, but we felt we were ready for the challenge to find out if we could bring our dreams to fulfillment.

Soon we learned that every moment things change, and most times you can't see change until it has happened. For example, during our celebration time together after marriage, we could not see the changes that would take place soon. While I returned to school for my last semester and Eligene to work, our fun time was reduced to weekends. Change was in the works.

At that very time without our awareness, although we should have been aware, four little angels were arguing in heaven about which one would come first to visit our home, bringing blessings. Ready or not, the first one was sent to us fourteen months after we said "I do." It was, as we discovered with joy, the first of four bundles of joy that we were to receive. When we were courting, we could not see the laughter and fun that would be ours from their antics, sometimes wild and sometimes plain crazy behavior.

Our children from oldest to youngest are: Lee Roy II, Eric Wayne, Jeanette Marie (Gina), and Darren Eugene. All of them are Pitts, and let the record show that I had these four and no more. And all four of them grew into independent, erudite and dialectical thinkers. Eligene and I take little credit for that, because it seems like it was not long before we were learning things from them, or they picked up on whatever new technology surfaced much faster than we did. There's so much stuff they did that we didn't know about that we had to laugh when we did find out. During their pre-teen years, they were our little rascals, as much of what they did was hilariously funny. You name what they were getting ready to do, right or wrong, and they could tell you which one of them would lead the charge.

It wasn't long before it seemed to me that Eligene was more prepared for all of the fast changes with children than I was. I just seem to have been prepared to work, do what she wanted, keep up with the children's school needs, and protect the family. I have a lot of catching up to do in regard to the family thing, because in the beginning I laughed at some of things the boys did that really weren't funny. Eligene seemed to just naturally know what to do. However, looking back and thinking about the upfront challenges such as the monetary struggle of family life, the time required, tears shed from seeing children hurt, goals that had to be put on hold, and all the other challenges, I believe the gift of our children was our greatest blessing, short of spiritual salvation.

After our first child, Lee Roy, was born, I recall Eligene praying for a daughter. She wanted a daughter very much. Our daughter Jeanette came in third. Since all of our children are leaders, any of them could have been first in the birth order. First, I would not have wanted Lee and Jeanette together during their preteen and teen years. Together they surely would have reinforced each other to do something crazy. Second, I would not have wanted Lee and Darren together, although they would not have been as problematic as Lee and Jeanette together. Eric would have been fine in any position as long as the above couples were not together. I know they will laugh when they see this, because they know better than Eligene and me who, when together, would have tended to throw all caution to the wind and who would tend to at least infuse a bit of wisdom.

So I now see four balanced adults, but I am so thankful that heaven knew best in what order to send them. I am reminded of the scripture that says, "But as it is written, eyes have not seen, nor ear heard, neither have entered into the heart of man, the things which God hath prepared for them that love him."

Before marriage how I remember praying about a wife who would be a good mother to my children. I hoped my children would be capable of learning and want to learn. Then I remember hoping they would be obedient, at least within the norm for children. I experienced so many of my wants that I call it nothing short of another Unexpected Encounter with Grace . Though we worked hard to help answer our prayers, I hoped for a wife who was of the same faith tradition as myself. After they started arriving with all their energy, I realized I should have asked for more energy for Eligene and me.

Through it all we experienced answered prayers beyond our expectations. Since then we see blessings overflowing to grand and great grandchildren. It is a blessing that our children have backgrounds where they are able to help others. Lee Roy attended Ottawa University, worked as a computer analyst, and now is an electrician at General Motors.

Eric Wayne graduated Yale and Washington University Medical School, and now is in private medical practice. Jeannette Marie graduated Stanford University, was inducted into Phi Beta Kappa, was a Rhodes scholar, and is now a Mohs Surgeon. Darren Eugene graduated Kansas State University and is now a pharmaceutical representative None of them have been before a judge for crimes. All are involved with helping people, tutoring, and other such helps. This is mentioned not to say how fortunate we have been as parents, for that is a given. It is mentioned so I can say to my grandchildren that along with your own Mom and Dad, you have aunts and uncles who are very capable of guiding and helping you excel enough so you do not have to fail at reaching your goals.

It did not take me long after marriage to know how blessed I was to have Eligene as my wife. She has been not only a good wife but an excellent mother to and for our children. Her positives are so many as to make negatives, from being herself, too few to dwell upon. I still am fascinated by some of the apparently odd things she does to solve some problems. Even when the method she uses seems ridiculous, I can't complain because somehow most of the crazy approaches she uses, work.

It soon became a fun saying of mine that God favored her over me. In short, it has been a good life with her. Even when I am upset with her, I still do not want to be out of her presence for very long. Regarding her as a mother, I cannot think or envision any girl I dated, liked, or loved, being as good a mother for our children as Eligene. She is a homemaker par excellence.

As a teacher I brought home less money from my main job than many other occupations. So often I left Northeast Junior for a part-time job. When I went to work in the

Metropolitan Community College District - Penn Valley College, I always worked an overload. That usually meant teaching a night class in addition to day classes. Also I never could afford to take a sabbatical because at one time we had three children in college. All of this allowed me to bring in more money. I can say Eligene never wasted our funds.

Even with less money, we managed to do the things that we valued most. We gave our tithes and offerings to our church. When we had building fund campaigns, we gave, and at the end of one campaign, we decided we would for some time continue to give for that purpose. Eligene didn't complain. When there were field trips scheduled at school and our children were sick, we sent the money to cover a child whose family was in need. The teachers knew our intent and took care. That was done by Eligene and that evening when told, I didn't complain. When I brought kids home to eat because I learned their family was in want of funds, Eligene fed them like they were our own and didn't complain. When we helped youngsters to get to college with money we had saved for something we needed, somehow it was made up. We stood by each other, and somewhere we felt like the hand of God was upon our efforts.

I confess that getting to or going to a heaven was not on my mind when we did what was helping either us or someone else. Rather I just knew there was a need and it is right to do right when and if you can.

Both of us knew that family life was hard work, and that unless we committed together, something would go awry and goals would not be met. Our goal and our commitment was to create an environment that would permit our children and other children to reach their maximum development physically, psychologically, and emotionally. In part our goals were derived from the fact that neither of us believed we had had environments that permitted us to develop to our potential or even approximating our potential. Especially is this true for my wife. I know she could have graduated college and grad school, such is her ability to reason and critically analyze. She is often heard to say, "Children deserve better," after seeing some behavior or language around growing children.

Knowing that raising children and staying with someone is hard work, there was one thing ever on my mind. I did not want to commit "malpractice" on my children. Malpractice is simply when you do not do the best you can. Knowing I wasn't going to be a perfect dad, I nevertheless wanted to do the best I could. This was rooted in the fact that I do not believe my dad did the best he could have done towards his family. Life is too short to repeat the mistakes of our family.

During early marriage Eligene was a stay-at-home mom. The children and I enjoyed her being there. I came home to the smell of a good meal cooking or ready. Sometimes she would be on the sewing machine. Whichever child was the baby at the time was well attended. How she did it all, I do not know to this day. I'm not the only husband to have discovered this in good mothers. When I stayed home with the children and though having stayed, I nonetheless felt like joining the French Foreign Legion. Eligene did it day after day and for a number of years.

Now after 53 years of marriage, four children, and many personal sacrifices for them and me, I tell Eligene often how much I love her and do what will make her know it. Our children love, cherish, and honor her also. She stuck with me and our family through good times and bad - a good mother and wife.

Anyone around me would know that to survey the peaks and valleys of my life, my joyous peaks came after marriage. Being with my family gave me real life. Whenever we did things that were to be fun for the children, I enjoyed it as much as our children did. Just to see them have fun was life enhancing for me. Things like walnut hunting, visiting the zoo, playing games at home in winter where they usually ganged up on me, having breakfast in the park when traveling to my sister Alberta and Uncle Eugene's in California, seeing the Grand Canyon together, seeing each of them get their driver's license and so much more, all added to my life.

Our children are so special to me because they knew that few men, especially Black men, can provide all that is wanted by children and at times have trouble providing necessary needs. However, our children honored and respected our efforts as Christian parents. For their awareness I am so grateful because they worked with us and sacrificed in many ways. They understood when we spread our love to others through giving. They are in my heart so much I would put my life on the line for any of them and Eligene.

Eligene and I feel wonderfully blessed to have had, not just children, but our children. As I look back, I can agree with Maya Angelou when she said, "I wouldn't take nothing for my journey now."

I have enjoyed many things and faced a number of challenges, but none have I loved more than putting my family's needs first. To provide for them, to help them develop sound values for life, to provide security, all were things I loved doing more than my life. My family was truly life-giving to me. Now I am receiving a double blessing as we receive love and attention from and give to our grand and great grandchildren.

CHAPTER XV

SERVANT YEARS

My spiritual pilgrimage and my servant work has its roots in the Black church. The spiritual or religious thought to which I was exposed came early in life since as children we had to go to some church every Sunday. Later when I went to military service, I met people on military bases who were of many religious faiths. A number of them I engaged in conversation about their faith. All of this caused me to entertain religious thoughts for the first time that before leaving home were foreign to me.

My Christian pilgrimage began under a caring minister and his wife, Elder Goff David Young and Sister Anna Mae Young. We addressed him in any of several ways: Elder Young, Reverend Young, or Brother Young. He was pastor of Third Street Church of God at 1907 North Third Street in Kansas City, Kansas. He was pastor there when I made the decision to accept Jesus Christ's way of living.

Those of us who were under his leadership saw in him the humility, wisdom, and concern for people seldom seen in many leaders. He was a strong gospel preacher who was excellent in preaching to the needs of people whose backs were against the wall, so to speak. He was focused always on helping through the Word of God and action to help people see and understand the will of God for their lives. Preaching the "Word" was so important to him that we never saw him "trivialize" preaching by "clowning" or "show boating" in the pulpit. He would not waste God's time or ours. Some of his greatest strengths were unselfishness and being aware of his weak areas in ministry. Knowing his weak areas allowed him to build strength where he was weak, and he could better bring help to the church. He often invited good preachers and teachers to minister to us.

I recall him inviting a minister by the name of Samuel G. Hines to preach. Reverend Hines ran a thirty-day revival, thirty straight days. Our choir sang every night. The church was full every night, and young and old were present. I remember it so clearly because under his preaching, my pilgrimage was moved to another level of commitment and insight. I do not believe I was alone in such commitment. There had to be levels of seriousness because this revival was in July, in Kansas. As Brother Hines said, "It was hot." Another great preacher and friend, pastor Ben Reid, speaking of Kansas, said, "Anyone who goes to hell from Kansas, deserves to go there." Kansas is that hot in July and August. I first became aware of expository form of preaching from Brother Hines, thanks to pastor Goff Young's foresight.

Many of us across the nation were given a foundation for service to the church by the leadership of Elder Goff Young and the pastor before him, Elder Gabriel Dixon.

Following Elder Young, Third Street called a young minister by the name of Sethard A. Beverly. Reverend Beverly was a recent graduate of our foremost Church of God College, Anderson University in Anderson, Indiana. He was married to one of Third Street's girls who came up under Pastor Young. Her name was Sandra Kathryn Doniphan, and she had gone to Ball State University in Indiana before her marriage to Sethard Beverly. She was one of my wife's childhood friends and closest church friend. Sister Beverly was a classmate of mine at Sumner High School in Kansas City, Kansas.

Reverend Beverly and I were recent graduates from college. Our wives were longtime close friends, and both families were just starting to have children, so it was an easy association that proved to be good for both families and the church. It was not long before to our children they were Uncle Seth and Aunt Sandy; conversely, we became Uncle Lee Roy and Aunt Gene to their children.

In matters of religious courses or theology at that time I had no formal courses other than philosophy and ethics. Seth had what amounted to little or no formal science courses beyond general college courses in biology. This background difference proved to be of much worth, since we saw the need to consult when needed. On more than one occasion he visited and sat in the back of my physical science class. I gave suggested science topics that would be of benefit to theology students or preachers. In turn, he made his library of seminary authors available to me and suggested theological topics that would be valuable to science majors. We were available to each other by way of periodic discussions; some were planned. We soon learned each other's weaknesses and strengths, which was of help in determining where best to use me and when.

When I was in college, many weekends I came home and taught Sunday School. When Seth came and college was over, I continued to teach and continued in the choir. Soon I was a trustee and served as chairman for almost ten years, also as a lay minister. Of them all, my heart was and remained as a teacher. Second to my love of teaching was my love of doing the work of a Deacon. I loved those two more than my life. Both of them involved looking at the needs of people and trying to build that bridge to solving concerns. I felt called to them both.

Reverend Beverly took the view that all Christians are ministers, and within that broadness are special callings. However, often we saw people use their special callings and gifts as an excuse not to do other jobs in the church which they could do, at least short time. Often in small churches, of necessity we had to do double duty. Therefore I credit Seth for getting me ready for service by preparing me to do tasks normally left to the special calling of preaching. Especially did he prepare me for handling funeral services. Years later when he was very ill, my readiness came in handy. He called one day and said, "Roy I am sick. I will preach the eulogy, but you'll have to take it from there." I did so, though I would have been nervous without his foresight. Then and still later after he had gone from Third Street and retired, others called me to eulogize their old family member who had been under Pastor Beverly. Again Reverend Beverly's belief in using people was useful to the church, and not just Third Street Church, since it has been my privilege to help at other churches.

There were other things that, because of my background, all he had to do was assign it to me. I considered myself an erudite and dialectical thinker. Seth appreciated that and used me in a number of ways, especially consultation, and I used him in consultation. In short, we became each other's "right hand" man. For me these were opportunities to serve people - through the church. For forty years I gave my best to Third Street Church of God. More than twenty of these were under Reverend Sethard Beverly's pastoral watch.

By far I was not alone in committed service to the church at that time. We were fortunate to have a number of talented people in key positions. Our music department was in the very capable hands of Dr. Edward Eddy, an educator, English professor, and then Dean at Rockhurst College, later a professor at Kansas University. Ed received excellent instruction from nationally known music teachers when at Sumner High School. He was in his own right a top vocalist and nationally known in our church movement. He brought all of that distinction to the church. The variety of music he brought to our church helped us become known as the church with good singing. More important to us, Ed was excellent at selecting songs that supported the sermons that were preached on whatever occasion. Dr. Eddy's service extended to many other churches. Supporting all that Dr. Eddy did was his wife, our sister Joyce Eddy.

My contribution to the choir, such as it was, was as a bass singer. I stood beside a real bass, and one of the best in the city, Brother Arnold Saunders. Brother Eddy brought such an eclectic mix of songs that singing was a joy and a learning experience for me. During holiday seasons, our church was blessed with great anthems like John W. Peterson's "Night of Miracles." Another positive contribution was the piano and vocal service of Sister Loretta Clark.

Fortunate also was the number of senior women and men who had been with the church since Pastor Young and a few since pastor Gabriel Dixon. Every department had one of these where one could go for guidance and suggestions. In music we had Sister Lydia Mae Jones, an old faithful who was a forerunner to Brother Eddy. There were about fifteen men and slightly more senior women who were as solid in the faith as you'll ever see. Their cooperation and financial contribution were the backbone of much of the success achieved in the church. When we remodeled and added to the church, they were there in every way. Some of my most cherished times were doing the remodeling phase.

Since Brother Eddy and I were off during summers, it was nothing for us to be at the church very late at night painting or doing some other task. I recall being there with Reverend Beverly, Brother Eddy, and Brother James Greene when soon would appear Brother David Saunders. David was a professional who more than likely stopped to check something on which he was working. There was such a unifying force, it made service fun for us young leaders.

Our own Brother Jeffrey Rush was our contractor when we remodeled. We also had on board another professional for consultation in Brother Emmitt Pulley and his wife, Sister Emma Pulley. I mentioned these brothers because they were my seniors, and I learned so much from them when I was chairperson of the Trustee Board. Their love and concern for the church and its future was seen in their actions.

Fortunately we were in the youth area during Reverend Beverly's pastorate to have Sister Beverly and Sister Howse. Sister Howse came to be affectionately called "Momma Howse." It says something about how the youth viewed her and what she was to them. Always there are a few folks who are so talented that they work equally well with all age groups. In our church and at that time that was true for some wonderful sisters - Lydia Mae Jones, Vannetta Greene, Bernadette Barber, Ethel Coleman, Joyce Eddy, Shirley Harland, Georgia Barry, Audrey Nesley and Arlene Young. Equally as valuable was Brother Stanley Saunders, or actually, any of the Saunders men.

We had a dear and precious sister who had taken classes at Carver Baptist Bible Institute and specialized in child evangelism. In that area I have seen none better. She was loved by us all. She worked with children from kindergarten to around third grade. This was none other than the one and only Sister Edith Hayden. She was truly our Mother Teresa.

My wife Eligene was teaching Sunday School when she was in high school. When Pastor Beverly came, there was a need for someone to give children's sermons. Inasmuch as Eligene was familiar with children's church that was active under Pastor Young, it was fitting for her to head that up. She took on the task, and for a number of years it was an asset to the church. Also she worked with me when we teamed up to present seminars on marriage enrichment for married couples. That was something I enjoyed because I could see some benefit, and reports from those attending were good.

When we began to remodel, one thing church members did not want to go slack was the preaching and our evangelistic fervor. I can say that Reverend Beverly's sermons continued to be tops, and the Women's Missionary Society did not allow the evangelistic fervor to dwindle.

All of the people whose names I have mentioned represent a time in Eligene's and my life when we were working with a group of the most wonderful people of God who truly were our brothers and sisters in deed. We knew we were standing on the shoulders of some of them, building on what they had done. For others, we hope we passed a baton to them in teaching them the necessity of being faithful to the cause of Christ.

I still marvel at how things worked out for the benefit of the church. When some of us had nearly come to the end of our energy resources, some of our young people were ready to step into leadership positions. This was true with Bro Ronald Harland and his wife, our sister Patricia. They took the baton further up the hill, so to speak Also during our building phase it was my joy to see my sons Lee Roy and

Eric with our other teenage boys, hanging from rafters, doing what us older ones could only do in our dreams. What a beautiful sight seeing older persons making way for younger ones to labor in the vineyard.

All of this I have talked about because the period was a part of my life where serving was such a joy; I am still grateful for the opportunity. The last time I spoke long distance with Seth, my pastor, my friend, my co-laborer in the Kingdom of God, he was suffering from physical concerns. I had recently done a favor for him on my end, and he was thanking me. I remember him saying thanks for the favor. He followed the thanks with the statement, "Roy, you are closer than my blood brother." I knew what my friend meant, where his heart was. At that time he was getting ready to get out of here to be with the Lord on the other side. His mind was still clear but his speech had to be short.

Briefly, the essence of our last talk that day was a quick rehash of things we had long since recognized and talked about. Regarding the work at the church, we had seen that we could have made some wiser decisions in some matters. For the most part and greater still was the fact that we did many things right as we served in and for the Lord's church. Even when we remodeled the building, we were not building so we could glory in the brick and mortar, but rather we wanted a building where more and better ministry - service to and for people - could be done. We wanted lives to be changed in accordance to what Jesus says was his purpose in coming: He said I have come that they may have life and that more abundantly.

It was not long after college that my servant work extended into the neighboring churches in the Kansas City metro area. I was invited and accepted speaking engagements and presented seminars to community organizations.

It was my privilege to have been invited to speak at both the Christian Methodist Episcopal and the African Methodist Episcopal conventions. I also made a contribution for community improvement through civic involvement in the 1960s and more recently by serving on the City Planning Commission. Then service by way of my fraternity - Alpha Phi Alpha - is close to my heart, as we work to stem teen pregnancies by working with young boys.

My preparation for service was not just one thing. First I was prepared early through the circumstance of working with my aunt as a pre-teen on. I went with her to take care of the sick. She would bathe them and change their bed linens, which she took home to wash. I would sweep or clean windows, empty the trash and the water pan under the ice box. I did not know then that that experience bent me in the direction of service and helping the people. In that sense I had little choice but to serve.

When I began to get serious about a Christian lifestyle, I was challenged by two things. One I read in a book that when the Lord calls each person, he calls us "to Belong to Him." The author then said, "When we belong to him we will do whatever we can to render service." I was just beginning my Christian walk and was gripped by the meaning behind the statement and could never shake it from my values and view of service.

Still later I was moved and challenged by the book, Jesus and the Disinherited by Dr. Howard Thurman. From it I was better prepared for service to those who stand with their backs against the wall - to those who have given up on hope.

It was Howard Thurman who caused me to love a life of service. I was fortunate to have teamed with Dr. Sethard Beverly, as we both saw the need in the neighborhood and around the church and realized the Lord called us to belong to him right there and at that time.

Since the early days under Pastor Gabriel Dixon, Third Street Church of God has always acted like a lighthouse, sending people out into the world like beacons of light. I thank God that my wife Eligene and I are part of that stream of people still trying to keep the torch of the Gospel burning bright.

We are completing our church service at Kansas City Community Church at 59th and Leavenworth Road under a gifted pastoral team. Bishop Richard and Carolyn Prim received us well and have found areas of ministry for us to serve at our age. They are a gifted couple who have a love for people, especially our youth. We are grateful that they are shepherding us in our senior years.

We are thankful for those gone on who gave us our foundation stones, and we thank God for counting us worthy to be his servant ambassadors while here.

EPILOGUE

CLOSING THOUGHTS

My entrance into the world was during the Great Depression of the 1920s and 1930s. Segregation in the United States was still in full bloom, north and south. With poverty widespread, it was no surprise that most people experienced the Depression to some degree. However, Afro-Americans like my folks felt the effects of both poverty and segregation. These effects were a constant in every sector of life. I knew and experienced it growing up. For whites, this was not the case, as they, from my perspective, felt that hurt off and on and only here and there.

In this brief telling of my life for my family, integrity demanded that I tell bits and pieces of all sides of my life experience. Given the fact that one can talk about some things in several contexts and it sounds different, I have on occasion repeated a few things I deemed important from one time period and another. I shared something of my early home life, how my home was without my dad present, about the neighborhood environment that was physically not the best for children - though we still had times of fun. I told about the tension at my aunt's house during my mid-teen years. I also talked about how we coped with segregation in college.

Then naturally I mentioned a number of people who had a positive influence on me. Lastly, I gladly and easily talked about the three loves of my life: namely, my occupation of teaching, my service to the church, and love of my family.

Regarding the adverse things I talked about, one could question why I would mention those when they are behind me at this juncture of my life. Believe me, I have not shared the adverse because I enjoy them, nor because I intend to dwell on the negative. Far from any of those. First, I mention them because not to tell that side would present a fractured, incomplete picture of my life. Then, while the negatives are behind me in time, their effects still reverberate in my memory cells. Inasmuch as the adverse is in my memory cells, I have used them to remind myself that since I overcame those obstacles back then, I can handle obstacles today. So I do what so often we must: look back - then go forward.

I am aware that too often in our past the Black male, before and during my time, looked back and dwelled there. That was not beneficial. Also, often when mistakes are made, they carry over to affect the next generation. I have tried to avoid that error, knowing that life is too short to keep repeating errors of our family. So I have tried to look back with purpose to go forward.

The lesson for my family is to study the past, be mindful of our errors, and use the knowledge as a beacon of light to minimize your own errors so you can better move forward. I think the generation of our family that raised me did a good job of preparing me to be able to right or minimize my errors. They did so when they gave me a moral compass based on the Christian Bible. Then very early I saw in our folks an ability to love people regardless of race or ethnicity.

The last thing I received from them that helps me to correct my errors is the knowledge of the need to be willing to forgive. More than a few times I heard Aunt Lydia say, "Just forgive and move on." When people cheated her on payment for washing clothes, she did just that - forgave and moved on. When they paid her she would do their clothes again, but not before.

Those three things I tried to practice because I still believe in them. I believe in the need for a moral compass based on a stable standard, and for us Christians, it is the Bible. I still believe that after becoming a New Man in Christ, it is possible to love people. Third, I still think the way to internal peace is through forgiveness.

So I pray that you, my family, will be challenged to love, to stay with a stable moral compass, and learn how to forgive. To share my beliefs about those three should help all of you to understand the times I went the extra mile in relations with a few people. Thank you for loving me as a dad when you may not have understood the driving mechanism within me. How I love you four.

To look back on my life, I see so clearly the Unexpected Encounters with Grace in so many ways. It has been like a Golden Strand of the love of God going before me. It causes a deep continuing spirit of gratefulness. I found His love to be awesome. I saw His love woven into my wife's mothering of our children and into her being a wife. It was visible as showers of blessings on our children, and now I have seen the showers on our children's children. Most of us know what we've seen, and for real I saw His love open doors that were closed before to me. I saw His love close doors of hatred that were meant for me.

When I look at my life and think about all that happened and the how of it all, two things seem to bring closure. They are one of my favorite poems and a favorite song.

The title of the poem is "Touch of the Master's Hand" by Myra Welsh. The song is "The Angel Song." These speak to my views of what got me where I am in thought and behavior today. To my children, you know where I stand, so to my grand and great grandchildren, when you can't see a way out of entanglements, give the God of the Bible a chance at guiding your life. His love and His way will make a difference. It did for me.

I love you all.

TOUCH OF
THE MASTER'S HAND

BY MYRA WELCH

Twas battered and scarred, and the auctioneer
Thought it scarcely worth his while
To waste much time on the old violin,
But held it up with a smile.

"What am I bidden, good folks," he cried,
"Who'll start the bidding for me?"
"A dollar, a dollar," then "Two!" "Only two?
Two dollars, and who'll make it three?"

"Three dollars, once; three dollars, twice;
Going for three…" But no,
From the room, far back, a gray-haired man
Came forward and picked up the bow.

Then, wiping the dust from the old violin,
And tightening the loose strings,
He played a melody pure and sweet
As a caroling angel sings.

The music ceased, and the auctioneer,
With a voice that was quiet and low,
Said: "What am I bid for the old violin?"
And he held it up with the bow.

"A thousand dollars, and who'll make it two?"
"Two thousand! And who'll make it three?"
"Three thousand, once; three thousand, twice;
And going and gone," said he.

The people cheered, but some of them cried,
"We do not understand What changed its worth?"
Swift came the reply:
"The touch of the master's hand."

And many a man with life out of tune,
And battered and scarred with sin,
Is auctioned cheap to a thoughtless crowd,
Much like the old violin.

A "mess of pottage," a glass of wine;
A game, and he travels on.
He is "going" once, and "going" twice,
He's "going" and almost "gone."

But the Master comes and the foolish crowd
Never can quite understand
The worth of a soul and the change that's wrought
By the touch of the Master's hand.

THE LOVE OF GOD

The love of God is greater far than tongue or pen can
    ever tell;
It goes beyond the highest star, and reaches to the lowest
    hell.
The guilty pair, bowed down with care, God gave his son to
    win;
His erring child He reconciled and pardoned from his sin.

When hoary time shall pass away, and earthly thrones and
    kingdoms fall,
When men, who here refuse to pray, on rocks and hills and
    mountains call,
God's love so sure, shall still endure, all measureless and
    strong;
Redeeming Grace to Adam's race the saints' and angels'
    song.

Could we with ink the ocean fill, and were the skies of
    parchment made,
Were every stalk on earth a quill, and every man a scribe by
    trade,
To write the love of God above would drain the ocean dry.
Nor could the scroll contain the whole, tho' stretched from
    sky to sky.

Chorus:
O love of God, how rich and pure! How measureless and
    strong!
It shall forevermore endure
    the saints' and angels' song.

REFERENCES CITED

Lanney, Naomi E., Ed.D. 2006. *The spirit of our children.* Overland Park, KS: Leathers Publishing.

Monroe, Charles R. 1975. *Profile of the community college.* San Francisco: Jossey Bass.

Peck, M. Scott, M.D. 1978. *The road less traveled.* New York: Simon and Schuster.

PROFILE

Lee Roy Pitts, son of Charlotte Lockridge and Miles Pitts, was born in the Kaw Valley District (West Bottoms) of Kansas City, Kansas. When he was five years of age, his mother died and he went to stay with his aunt and uncle, Lydia and Isom Love. There he lived with his four siblings, Alberta and Albert (twins), Madeline, and Evelyn until his late teens.

Lee Roy Pitts, Sr.

He served in the military during the Korean War and received several decorations: the United Nations Medal, Korean Service Medal with two Bronze Stars, Japan Occupation Medal, a Presidential Unit Citation, and the Good Conduct Medal. He received an Honorable Discharge.

After military service, he used his training as a Cartographer while working for the Corps of Engineers (Army Map Service) as a Cartographic Draftsman. It was there that he saw the need for a broader educational experience.

Lee Roy earned the Bachelor and Masters degree in

Biological Science from Pittsburg State University in Pittsburg, Kansas, and the Doctor of Philosophy from Louisiana Baptist University and Theological Seminary. He did advanced science work at the University of Colorado and Kansas State University. He received his Counseling Certification by attending Central Missouri State University in Warrensburg, Missouri.

His teaching career began at Northeast Junior High School in 1958. There he served as Chairperson of the Science Department and teacher of freshman General Science and Biology. Later he served as a school counselor. In 1972 he took a position at the Metropolitan Community Colleges, Penn Valley Community College as Biology teacher and later served as Chairperson of the Biology Department.

Lee Roy married Eligene Clay (Sumner Class of 1953) in 1956. They have three sons: Lee Roy, Eric Wayne, M.D., and Darren Eugene; and one daughter, Jeanette Marie (Gina), M.D. They have six grandchildren.

Lee Roy has served the Kansas City metropolitan area in a number of ways. For forty years he served at the Third Street Church of God as Sunday School Teacher, choir member, deacon, Chairperson of Trustee Board, and lay minister. His service has extended to other churches and organizations. He is a member of Kansas City Community Church and Alpha Phi Alpha Fraternity. He was active in civic affairs during the 1960s and in recent years served on the City Planning Committee.

He is a member of the Sumner Alumni Association, the NAACP, and a number of professional organizations.

Author contact information:

Lee Roy Pitts Sr., PhD.
8016 Corona Avenue
Kansas City, Kansas 66112
913-788-3265